Socrates,
Pleasure,
and
Value

Socrates,
Pleasure,
and
Value

George Rudebusch

New York   Oxford
Oxford University Press
1999

Oxford University Press

Oxford   New York

Athens   Auckland   Bangkok   Bogotá   Buenos Aires   Calcutta
Cape Town   Chennai   Dar es Salaam   Delhi   Florence   Hong Kong   Istanbul
Karachi   Kuala Lumpur   Madrid   Melbourne   Mexico City   Mumbai
Nairobi   Paris   São Paulo   Singapore   Taipei   Tokyo   Toronto   Warsaw

and associated companies in
Berlin   Ibadan

Copyright © 1999 by George Rudebusch

Published by Oxford University Press, Inc.
198 Madison Avenue, New York, New York 10016

Oxford is a registered trademark of Oxford University Press

Library of Congress Cataloging-in-Publication Data
Rudebusch, George, 1957–
Socrates, pleasure, and value / George Rudebusch.
p.   cm.
Includes bibliographical references and index.
ISBN 0-19-512855-9
1. Socrates.   2. Ethics, Ancient.   3. Pleasure.
4. Hedonism
I. Title
B318.E8R83   1999

183'.2—dc21   98-36534

1 3 5 7 9 8 6 4 2

Printed in the United States of America
on acid-free paper

To
M.R.
L.R.

My greatest pleasure is to hear and to speak about Socrates, remembering him.

Plato, *Phaedo* 58d

Preface

This book interprets and evaluates arguments given by Socrates in dialogues written by Plato, in particular, those Socratic arguments needed to solve an interpretive puzzle: does Socrates believe pleasure or virtue is the supreme good? These Socratic texts and issues are of basic interest to the study of Plato, pleasure, or prudential value. All Greek has been translated and transliterated (by me or as noted).

I do not consider all of Socrates' arguments or all of his ethics. In particular, I leave for another book a discussion of the problems arising from Socrates' equation of virtue with some kind of knowledge. I have merely tried to solve one basic problem for Socratic ethical theory, a problem so basic that it has led many to doubt there is a coherent account to be found. But my aim of solving a scholar's puzzle is also a grander aim: to open the eyes of you, Plato's reader, to whatever force his written arguments may have, in such a way that the arguments may cause your soul to begin, if not to advance in virtue and wisdom, at least to desire and seek them for their true value. The Delphic oracle pronounced Socrates the wisest of human beings. Let us, in studying Socrates' arguments, consider the experience of Alcibiades, who said, "His arguments were exactly like those hollow statues of Silenus that open down the middle. Anyone listening

to Socrates for the first time would find his arguments simply laughable. . . . But if you see them when they open up like the statues, if you
get inside of them, you'll find them to be the only arguments that make
sense, the most godlike in value" (*Symposium* 221e–222a, trans. after Joyce,
Nehamas and Woodruff).

Acknowledgments

Parts of the writing of this book were supported by summer research stipends from Northern Arizona University in 1989, 1992, and 1993, and from the National Endowment for the Humanities in the summer of 1992. I have presented and published earlier versions of portions of this book in many places; I thank in particular the departments of Philosophy at the University of Hawaii at Manoa and at Northern Arizona University for their collegiality and colloquia. There are a great many people to thank for encouragement, suggestions, and criticism, including Hope Lindsay Rudebusch, Susan Sauvé Meyer, and Gerasimos Santas, who read and criticized the entire manuscript at a near-final stage, the latter two as referees for Oxford University Press.

This work, seen as one speech in a lengthy conversation in letters, owes much to its interlocutors: all those I reference and discuss in the text and notes. I also acknowledge the following help on specific chapters. Thanks to David Sherry and Richard Wood for helpful comments on an earlier draft of chapter 2. An earlier version of chapter 4 was read and was the object of discussion at the 1990 Pacific Division Meeting of the American Philosophical Association, for which attention I am grateful; I also wish to thank the referees and editor of *Ancient Philosophy*, and Mike

Malone, Richard Wood, and Charles Young for helpful comments on chapter 4. Earlier versions of portions of chapter 5 were read and were the object of discussion at the 1988 Pacific and Central Division Meetings of the American Philosophical Association, for which attention I am grateful. I thank Scott Berman, Irwin Goldstein, Norman Mooradian, Fernando Muniz, Naomi Reshotko, Daniel C. Russell, and the audience at the 1997 Arizona Plato Colloquium for helpful comments on chapter 7. I thank Julia Annas, Scott Berman, Rick Creath, Peter Kosso, David Reeve, Dennis Rusche, David Sherry, Mike White, and the editor and anonymous referee of *History of Philosophy Quarterly* for helpful comments on portions of earlier drafts of chapter 8. An earlier version of chapter 10 was read and was the object of discussion at a Symposium on Socratic Philosophy at the 1994 Conference of the Society for the Study of Islamic Philosophy and Science and the Society for Ancient Greek Philosophy and at the 1995 Pacific Division Meeting of the American Philosophical Association, for which attention I am grateful; I thank in particular the commentator at the latter session, Debra Nails.

For professional encouragement and general support, I owe additional debts to Julia Annas, Margaret P. Battin, Hugh Benson, Scott Berman, Scott W. Calef, Antonio K. Chu, Darrel D. Colson, Irwin Goldstein, Richard Kraut, Lila Luce, Fernando Muniz, Ronald Polansky, Anthony Preus, Andrew J. Reck, Naomi Reshotko, David C. Ring, Daniel C. Russell, Shyrley Souza, and Charles Young. Mark McPherran and Nicholas D. Smith have been like big brothers to me in their philosophical support through criticism, advice, and encouragement. Many will recognize this work as belonging to a student of Terry Penner. Thanks to the University of Wisconsin at Madison and his able colleagues, I received from him metaphysical views and exegetical skills as well as instruction on particular texts that marked me, indeed made me, as a philosopher. But the errors of this work are mine alone.

The following chapters use revised versions of previously published work. I am grateful to these journals and publishers and their editors for their permission so to use.

Chapter 2: "Plato's Aporetic Style," *Southern Journal of Philosophy* 27, no. 4 (1989): 539–547. Reprinted in *Plato: Critical Assessments*, vol. 1, ed. Nicholas D. Smith (New York: Routledge, 1998).

Chapter 3: "Plato, Hedonism, and Ethical Protagoreanism," in *Essays in Ancient Greek Philosophy*, vol. 3, eds. John Anton and Anthony Preus (Albany: State University of New York Press, 1989), 27–40.

Chapter 4: "Callicles' Hedonism," *Ancient Philosophy* 12, no. 1 (1992): 53–71.

Chapter 6: "Death Is One of Two Things," *Ancient Philosophy* 11, no. 1 (Spring 1991): 35–45.

Chapter 8: "The Righteous Are Happy," *History of Philosophy Quarterly* 15, no. 2 (April 1998): 143–160.

Chapter 10: "How Socrates Can Make Both Pleasure and Virtue the Chief Good," *Journal of Neoplatonic Studies* 3, no. 1 (1994): 163–177.

Flagstaff, Arizona   G.R.
March 1999

Contents

Note on Abbreviations and Texts

I sometimes cite works of Plato, other ancient authors, and well-known modern authors (such as Hume) by abbreviated titles. Full titles are given in the index of passages. I cite Plato by the standard Stephanus pages and lines, using the Oxford classical text edited by Burnet (1900–1907). Other works I cite by author's name and date; they are listed in the bibliography.

Socrates,
Pleasure,
and
Value

ONE

Introduction

In the early dialogues of Plato, there seems to be an incoherent portrait of Socrates. He seems in the *Apology* and *Crito* to make virtue the supreme good in human life, but in the *Protagoras* to make pleasure that supreme good, yet in the *Gorgias* to deny that pleasure is the supreme good. This book reconciles the hedonist of the *Protagoras* with the anti-hedonist of the *Gorgias* by distinguishing two theories of pleasure: Socrates argues against one but accepts the other. It reconciles Socrates the (properly understood) hedonist with Socrates the virtue supremacist of the *Apology* and *Crito* by showing how Socrates can identify pleasant activity (according to his theory of pleasure) with virtuous activity. It is part of my project to provide a deeper philosophical understanding of Socrates' ideas that virtue is sufficient for happiness, that nothing bad can happen to a good man (*Ap.* 41d1). Such ideas can cause a fundamental change in one's life. On the strength of Socratic argument, I believe such ideas should be given serious consideration.

1.1 Overview

Plato's Socratic dialogues on the nature of virtue, knowledge, and the good life stand at the beginning of Western ethical thought.[1] Yet basic questions about these dialogues remain unsettled. This is in large part due to the fact that they are full of apparent inconsistencies. For example, Socrates appears in the *Apology* to be willing to break the law; in the *Crito* unwilling. Inconsistencies such as these lead some to conclude that there is no coherent theory underlying these dialogues, that they are not to be seen as arguing for an implicit positive doctrine.[2] But a majority of scholars think it reasonable to seek a plausible ethical theory in these dialogues.[3]

Probably the most divisive of the unsettled questions concerns the issue of hedonism, the doctrine that all good and evil, in the last analysis, is a matter of pleasure and pain. There is an astonishing split of scholars over whether the Socrates portrayed in these dialogues is a hedonist.[4]

Yet the hedonism issue is so basic that without resolving it in some satisfactory way an assessment of the place of the Socratic dialogues in the history of philosophy cannot be made. For without such a resolution it is difficult to know whether to place Socrates in the Stoic and Kantian ethical tradition, which postulates an absolute value for virtue apart from pleasure, or in the Epicurean and Utilitarian tradition, which allows virtue only the value of a means that happens to produce what an individual wants.[5] By interpreting and defending the thesis that pleasure and virtue are the same in human activity, I place Socrates outside both traditions.[6]

1.2 The Dialogue Style

Some of the Socratic dialogues refute various theses but end with no thesis endorsed. Such dialogues raise a problem: if these dialogues are meant to convey positive theses, why does Socrates not explicitly state them? Chapter 2 aims to solve this problem by finding a pedagogical motive for such dialogues. Pedagogically, to give a student or reader a mere slogan instead of comprehensive understanding accomplishes nothing good and risks causing something bad. Plato, aware of this, gives the reader the means for understanding (in the coils of the arguments he lays out) but few explicit slogans. If there are positive theses in the dialogues, there is a point to looking for coherence among them.

1.3 The Defense and Refutation of Hedonism

In the *Protagoras*, Socrates defends hedonism as a premise in an argument whose conclusion he accepts. He allows the people with whom he is talking to take him as accepting that premise himself. Thus it is natural to conclude on the basis of the *Protagoras* that Socrates is a hedonist. But there is a problem with this natural conclusion. In the *Gorgias*, Socrates attacks and refutes hedonism. Chapters 3 through 5 solve this problem by showing that what Socrates refutes in the *Gorgias* is a different species of hedonism from what he defends in the *Protagoras*.[7] In this way the apparent conflict between these dialogues disappears.

1.4 Virtue or Pleasure?

A distinction between two species of hedonism, only one of which Socrates defends, still leaves a problem. In the *Protagoras*, Socrates defends the claim that pleasure is the only good. But in the *Apology* and elsewhere Socrates unquestionably believes that virtue is a good above all others. Socrates cannot, it seems, have it both ways. Either virtue, as in the *Apology*, or pleasure, as in the *Protagoras*, may be the supreme good—but not both. Since the supremacy of virtue is unquestionable for Socrates, it would seem that hedonism is an impossible doctrine for Socrates to hold.

My solution to this problem is to interpret and defend a Socratic account of pleasure. Pleasure, in English as in Greek, is spoken of in two ways. I may speak of the pleasure I get from various activities. In this manner of speaking, pleasure is a *sensation*. I may also speak of a person's pleasures. In this manner of speaking, pleasure is a *mode* of activity, that is, an activity done in a certain way—one which is anticipated, which absorbs one's attention without effort, from which one is reluctant to break off—but which need not be associated with any sensations in particular. For example, a tennis player may enjoy intensely the activity of a match, yet—owing to chronic disease or injury—feel predominately or only sensations of pain while playing. I have mentioned some of the symptoms of *modal* pleasures—anticipation, absorption, unwillingness to break off—but Aristotle identified the reason why modal pleasures have these symptoms: they are essentially "unimpeded activities of the soul," which may be understood as the exercise of a capacity central to doing well as a human being.[8]

The *Apology* gives us grounds for ascribing a modal notion of pleasure to Socrates. There Socrates argues that dreamless sleep—a sensationless activity—is a surpassing pleasure (40d6). If Socrates held a sensate account of pleasure, such a claim would be laughably false (as indeed it has seemed to sensatist interpreters).[9] But, with a modal account of pleasure, a defense can be given of this Socratic argument. As I argue in chapter 6, dreamless sleep happens effortlessly and without boredom; one can approach it with anticipation and be reluctant to break off from it; it plays a meaningful role in life by relieving worries and pains as well as being refreshing. Though not a phenomenal event, it certainly may be unimpeded. And, as I argue in chapter 7, a modal account of pleasure captures what is valuable in pleasure, despite our attraction to the sensations of pleasure.

1.5 A Modal Account of Pleasure Allows Socrates to Identify Pleasant Activity with One Kind of Skillful Activity

Following Aristotle, I can say that a modal pleasure is an unimpeded activity in accordance with the nature of one's condition. If it is the nature of one's condition to be skillful (as, for example, in the case of a carpenter or weaver), then the activity in accordance with that nature will be the exercise of that skill (working with wood or weaving). Two cases need to be distinguished. Sometimes we do a skillful activity for its own sake; sometimes for the sake of something else.[10] In the second case, weaving is done in subordination to a superordinate goal, perhaps money or repair. In this case there is no reason to suppose the action displays the symptoms of or is a modal pleasure. Indeed, strictly speaking, the person who engages in this activity, however skillfully, only for subordinate reasons, is more properly called by the name of the superordinate skill: moneymaker or home economist.[11] But in the first case, the weaving would be done as a leisure activity freely chosen. One might weave without needing the weaved product; one might weave even in neglect of pressing needs. In such cases the activity of weaving is not toil for some superordinate necessity but is an expression of one's nature as a weaver. Pleasant activity for a weaver in this sense is nothing but the skillful activity of weaving. Weaving is an illustration; in general, this identity holds true for any insubordinate skillful activity.

1.6 A Modal Account of Pleasure Allows Socrates to Identify Pleasant Activity with Virtuous Activity

There is no question that for Socrates virtue is a matter of skill, not will (*Euthyd.* 278e–282e, *Meno* 77b–78b). And, while it is conceivable that one may perform a virtuous action for the sake of something else, such as prestige or money, a virtuous person, strictly speaking, chooses virtue in subordination to nothing else (*Ap.* 28b5–9, *Cri.* 48b–d). A virtuous person will accordingly freely choose to do virtuous activities. Because virtuous activities express one's nature without impediment, they display the symptoms of and are modal pleasures. Lest such a view seem too otherworldly to attribute to Socrates, notice that even this-worldly Aristotle holds that virtuous activity is necessarily pleasant to the virtuous person (*NE* 1099a7–21).

1.7 Socratic Argument Entails That, for a Human Being, Living Well, Living Pleasantly, and Living Virtuously Are One and the Same

Just as the distinctive excellence of a weaver is weaving, Socrates argues that the distinctive excellence of a human being is virtue (*Rep.* I 353e7–8; also see chapter 8 of this book for a defense of the argument). It follows that modal pleasure for a human being is unimpeded virtuous activity. Socrates can conclude that the virtuous person will necessarily live profitably and pleasantly.

1.8 Conclusion

The thesis of this book is that the Socrates of the *Apology*, *Crito*, *Protagoras*, *Gorgias*, and *Republic* I consistently and compellingly can speak of pleasure and virtue as the good for human beings by identifying pleasant with virtuous activity for a human being (chapter 10). This thesis follows from the following premises. Socrates (in the *Protagoras* and *Gorgias*) consistently and compellingly can speak of pleasure as the good for human beings (chapters 3–5). Socrates' hedonism can be interpreted to be a compelling theory of modal, not sensate, pleasure (chapters 6–7). Socrates (in the *Apology*, *Crito*, *Gorgias*, and *Republic* I) consistently and compellingly can speak of virtue as the good for human beings (chapters 8–9). Chapter 2 does not directly supply a premise supporting my thesis but defends the method of interpretation used throughout the book.

Plato's Aporetic Style

The written dialogue serves many purposes for Plato—artistic, ironic, and biographical, as well as philosophical. Perhaps the most important philosophical purpose is that an assumption central to Plato's philosophical mission—that human action of a certain sort presupposes the existence of philosophical endeavor if not knowledge—is well supported by the dialogue form, especially when it takes place in a setting between Socrates and a non-philosopher (such as a youth or general) or an anti-philosopher (such as a rhetor or sophist).[1] In addition, the dramatic details—such as date, place, names, and personalities of characters, and nesting of conversations within conversations—in many other ways enrich the philosophical content of a given dialogue.[2]

Neither Plato nor I believe philosophical understanding, even of so modest a nature as Socrates elicits, can be well taught merely by a written exposition of premises and inferences. (Written exchanges of objection and reply are another, more vital, matter.) One-way expository writing is dead in a way that conversation is alive (*Phdr.* 276e). One purpose of the dramatic context is to show that the premises used in the argument were particular to a discussion with particular interlocutors.[3] Some of the objections raised in a dialogue may not occur to the reader, while some that occur to the reader may not occur in the drama. In this book the nearest parallel to Socrates' interlocutors are the scholars cited in text and notes. Their objections and the reader's may overlap but probably are not identical. However, my concern in this chapter is to show how the puzzlelike ("aporetic") structure of certain dialogues—their ending in perplexity— helps Plato in yet another way toward the pedagogical goal of producing in his reader the understanding of Socrates' own philosophical position within those dialogues.[4] In what follows I shall describe one pattern I see in aporetic dialogues, and then explain that pattern by showing how it serves a pedagogical purpose better than more straightforward styles of expository writing. If my explanation is correct, then I have justified the method of interpretation that I describe in the conclusion of this chapter and use throughout this book.

There has been a persistent controversy over whether the aporetic dialogues are meant to convey any underlying philosophical position at all.[5] Both sides of the controversy agree that the author uses perplexity ("aporia") in its various forms to serve a purifying ("cathartic") purpose: the elimination of the conceit of wisdom in readers by refuting their words insofar as they can participate in the dialogue. But one side affirms while the other denies that there is also an elicitory ("maieutic") purpose: to elicit from the reader an understanding of a positive philosophical position.

Christian Brandis (1835: 159), quoted with approval by Eduard Zeller (1888: 157), provides a landmark statement of the maieutic side:

> Why should there so often be found in [the dialogues], after the destruction of imaginary knowledge by the essentially Socratic method of proving ignorance, only isolated and apparently unconnected lines of enquiry? why should some of these be hidden by others? why should the argument at last resolve itself in apparent contradictions? unless Plato presupposes his reader to be capable of completing by his own active participation what is wanting in any given enquiry, of discovering the central point in that enquiry, and of subordinating all the rest to that one point—presupposes also that only such a reader will attain any conviction of having understood at all.[6]

George Grote (1865: 292–299) is a landmark on the non-maieutic side:

> Interpreters sift with microscopic accuracy the negative dialogues of Plato, in hopes of detecting the ultimate elements of that positive solution which he is supposed to have lodged therein, and which, when found, may be put together so as to clear up all the antecedent difficulties. . . . I cannot take this view either of Socrates or of Plato.[7]

The non-maieutic reading has been accepted by some esoterists, those who distinguish between Plato's written and unwritten doctrine.[8] A strong argument in favor of the non-maieutic interpretation rests on this premise: if Plato had been trying to present a positive doctrine in his aporetic dialogues, he would have chosen a more straightforward style of writing for his purpose. I shall argue that this premise is false.

2.1 A Pattern in Aporetic Dialogue

Readers do not tend to wonder at the writing of Aristotle, Augustine, Descartes, or Berkeley in the way that they wonder at some of Plato's. This is because they all share what we might call a straightforward expository pattern of writing. Even when set out in a condensed, confessional, meditative, or dialectical way, they all may be seen as taking up a question and taking the reader step by step through some train of reasoning to an answer. Insofar as the writing is free of obscurity, it is a straightforward matter to identify the answer and the supporting account. We may not understand the explanation, but it is usually clear what the answer is, be it "Form is matter actually," "I think therefore I am," or "Evil (or material substance) does not exist." Some of Plato's dialogues are of the same straightforward sort. They set out an account that supports some answer, which is explicitly stated, usually in a single sentence.

However, the aporetic dialogues are different. A common pattern in the aporetic dialogues is to likewise begin with a question and then work step by step to an answer. But then that answer is undermined and rejected. For example, the *Laches* takes up the question "What is courage?" (190d–e). It provides an explanation in support of the answer, "Courage is knowledge of the hopeful and fearful" (195a, 195d–197b). But then it goes on to present a problem for and finally to abandon this answer (198a ff., esp. 199e). As another example, the *Meno* takes up the question "What is virtue?" (87d–e). It produces an explanation in support of the answer "Virtue is knowledge" (87d–e). But then it goes on to present a problem for and finally abandon this answer (89c–e and ff.).

These two examples are good starting points, because in both cases there is a scholarly consensus that Socrates accepts the answer that is explicitly rejected. This pattern can also be found in a majority of the other aporetic dialogues. In the *Lysis* the question arises, "What is a friend?" (212a; see also 223a); the answer elicited is "that which is neither good nor evil is friendly with the good because of the presence of evil" (218b–c); it is abandoned at 221d ff. In the *Euthyphro* the question is "What is piety?" (5d); the first answer—"The service of the gods" (12d with 13c)—is rejected at 14b; the second answer—"The science of giving and taking from the gods" (14d)—is rejected at 15a. In the *Charmides* the question is "What is temperance?" (159a); various answers are given (161b, 163e, 165b), including the most Socratic-sounding: "Temperance is the knowledge of good and evil," which is abandoned in the end (174d–175a). In the *Hippias Major* the question is "What is the fine?" (286c–d); various more or less Socratic answers are given and rejected (293e with 294d–e, 295c with 296d, 296e with 297d, and 297e–298a with 303d). The *Hippias Minor* contains what might be called a degenerate instance of this same pattern. The answer reached is immediately undermined, because it contradicts a widely accepted belief. The question there is, "Who are better, those who do wrong intentionally or unintentionally?" (371e–372a). The answer, "The intentional wrongdoer is better," is reached at 376b and immediately rejected. In the *Protagoras* one question is "Is virtue's unity more like the unity of a face or of a piece of gold?" (329d); the Socratic answer, "Virtue is all one knowledge," is argued for at length only to be disparaged in the end (361a–b). In each of these cases it is arguable, though I cannot give each argument here, that there is a way to understand the answers in a way with which Socrates would agree: I confine myself to the cases of the *Laches* and *Meno*.[9]

2.2 The Pedagogical Advantage of Aporia

What is the point of this pattern of first arguing for, then posing a problem and rejecting, a thesis that in likelihood was held by the author? Plato has left us with a clue to his design in a passage in which he spells out a criticism of other philosophers' ways of presenting their views. In the *Sophist* (242c–243d), the Stranger says that Parmenides and others "have used language too easily." His point seems to be that the writings of Parmenides and others do not really help us to understand their positions: "They overlooked most of us far too much; they had no consideration. For each one reasoned out his own argument without caring whether we follow or are left behind" (243a–b). It is clear how this criticism applies to an aphoristic style, which announces a one-sentence answer but does not show the reasoning behind the answer. As Socrates complains in the *Theaetetus*: "When you put a question, they pluck from their quiver little oracular aphorisms to let fly at you, and if you try to obtain some account of their meaning, you will be instantly transfixed by another, barbed with some newly forged metaphor" (180a, trans. Cornford).

Plato, to be sure, rightly saw that there is no gain in teaching someone to spout some slogan, if that person does not understand the reasoning of

which those words are a part.[10] In the language of the *Meno*, words without a tether will walk off; they are as hard to keep as a statue made by
Daedalus: "If no one ties them down, they run away and escape. If tied,
they stay where they are put. . . . [Thus] if you have one of his works
untethered, it is not worth much; it gives you the slip like a runaway slave.
But a tethered specimen is very valuable, for they are magnificent creations"
(97d–98b, trans. Guthrie; see also *Euthphr.* 11b–d and 15b). It can even
happen that the same slogan is affirmed by positions that are deeply opposed: both Socrates, as I interpret him, and Callicles affirm the identity
of pleasure and virtue, and both Socrates and Thrasymachus affirm the
excellence of the most profitable life. For this reason Plato has particular
reason to make clear the whole position behind the slogan, what the one
who said the slogan really had in mind (*Soph.* 243d), and was likely to see
the risk in teaching an incompletely understood slogan. (In addition to
pedagogy, there is apology: not a slogan, but only a more thoroughgoing
understanding, can enable Plato to achieve his apologetic goal in the dialogues of showing that Socrates is the truly pious and Euthyphro, Meletus,
and many jurors the falsely pious; Socrates the truly and Thrasymachus
the falsely powerful; Socrates the truly and Callicles the falsely satisfied;
and likewise with many other interlocutors.)

The pedagogical (and apologetic) goal may explain why Plato did not
write in aphorisms. But they do not yet explain why he chose the aporetic
pattern rather than a straightforward expository style. To see why he did
not settle for exposition, a distinction needs to be made and a picture
drawn. The distinction is between "single" and "double" ignorance. The
singly ignorant person is he who is ignorant but at least recognizes his
ignorance; the doubly ignorant person is he who, besides his ignorance,
takes himself to know, so he is ignorant of his ignorance, too. The dialogues, early, middle, and late (for example at *Ap.* 23a-b, *Meno* 84a-b, and
Tht. 210b-c), point out that one who is aware of one's ignorance is in a
better position to learn the truth than one taking oneself to know. It follows, I claim, that the dialogue will be either as good as or better than an
exposition along the same lines, depending on the particular reader. Just
how this claim is true can be seen in the following picture of the Socratic
dialogues.[11]

In each dialogue there is a teacher and a student. The teacher elicits
from the student an understanding of a one-sentence answer midway
through the dialogue. Then the teacher further examines the student. In
that examination, some problem with the student's understanding of the
whole position beneath the one-sentence answer will be uncovered and
used to undermine that answer. The dialogue ends, but now it is up to
the student and reader to "fight through" the various difficulties (this

"fight" is made a condition of knowledge at *Rep.* VII 534b–c). There are two cases to consider. If the student—and this applies as well to the reader—spots the problems that led to his rejecting the one-sentence answer, he will again be able to hold that answer, but with a better understanding of the whole position beneath it. In this case, the dialogue will be as good as the exposition; such a student or reader will gain the same insight into the account in either of the two forms in which it might be presented. On the other hand, if the student or reader does *not* spot the problem, at least he will be better off than if he had been given a straightforward exposition—for in that case he would not have understood the position but thought that he did; in the case of the dialogue he at least will be aware that he does not understand.

The problem with expositions is that, after they announce a one-sentence answer, they do not test the student for understanding. Plato believed that much further questioning is necessary even after the right one-sentence answer has been exposed. About the slave boy, after his "recollecting" a geometrical demonstration, Socrates says:

> At present these opinions, being newly aroused, have a dreamlike quality. But if the same questions are put to him on many occasions and in different ways, you can see that in the end he will have a knowledge on the subject as accurate as anybody's. (*Meno* 85c–d, trans. Guthrie; see also *Rep.* VII 534b–c)

It remains for me to show that this picture is drawn accurately. I shall consider in more detail the examples I took above.

Suppose that the question is "What is courage?" In the *Laches*, the student, Nicias, announces his one-sentence answer that courage is the knowledge of what is to be hoped for and feared (195a). Nicias has some understanding of the whole position that goes along with this answer. He denies that courage is one thing and wisdom another (195a). He is able to distinguish between the courageous person's knowledge of dangers and benefits and each other scientist's knowledge of dangers in their own areas (196b–d), even the soothsayer's (190e–196a). He does not call lions, leopards, or boars courageous, but only fearless, that is, devoid of the understanding of danger (196e–197b). But—and this is the root of his problem—he takes it that courage is *only* a part, along with many other parts, of virtue (198a). The problem develops as follows. He has to agree that courage is not only the knowledge of the fearful and hopeful (which lie in the future), but of good and evil things without reference to time (199c; see also 198d ff.). But in that case, he must also grant that the courageous person must lack no part of virtue; courage, instead of being only a part of virtue, will be all of virtue (199d–e). This contradiction tells Nicias that he has not discovered what courage is (199e); he did not have the (whole) answer. But the problem is not in Nicias's one-sentence answer; rather, his understanding of the whole position supporting that answer is lacking, for he thinks that courage is only a part of virtue. If he had argued that courage is indeed the whole of virtue, as is justice, piety, temperance, and wisdom, that is, that those five words stand for a single thing (as Socrates suggests at *Prt.* 349a–b), he would have avoided the problem.

The *Laches* fits the picture I drew. The student had the right one-sentence answer, but that was not enough. His own lack of understanding, his not seeing the whole position that goes along with his answer, forced him to deny the one-sentence answer. But the perplexity in which he was left made him less sure that courage is only one part of virtue. When or if he comes to accept the unity of virtue, he will again be able to assert his right one-sentence answer, but—what is important—with better understanding. Until then he is better off than if Socrates had treated him to a spoken exposition rather than a spoken dialogue. For an exposition would have left him not with better understanding but the harmful conceit of understanding. And the uncomprehending reader likewise is better off than if Plato had treated him to written exposition rather than written dialogue. On the other hand, the comprehending reader who succeeds in fighting through the difficulties will have profited as much from the Socratic dialogue as he would have from a written exposition along the same lines.

In the *Meno* the question is "What is virtue?" Meno reaches the one-sentence answer that virtue is knowledge (88c–e). But his problem begins when he allows that if anything is a knowledge (or science), there must be teachers of it (89d). For further arguments force him to grant that there are no teachers of virtue: neither Themistocles, nor Aristides, nor Pericles, nor Thucydides (93d–94d); nor any other typical, decent Athenian citizen (contrary to the suggestion at 92e); nor any among the fine characters of Meno's own homeland (95a–b); nor even among sophists (95c, 96a–b). So he must give up his one-sentence answer that virtue is knowledge. Meno is left perplexed at the end. But if he ever comes to question his assumption that there are at least some competent teachers for every knowledge (or science), if he ever decided that perhaps *everyone* is ignorant of the knowledge of virtue (as Socrates believed, *Ap.* 23a–b), then he may once again assert his right one-sentence answer, but—and this is what matters for Plato—with better understanding. Again, both Meno and the uncomprehending reader are better off than if they had been treated to a spoken or written exposition, respectively. And the compre-

hending reader profits as much from a written dialogue as from a written
exposition.

Bishop Butler took a similar view of how one ought to present philosophy: "I have often wished that it had been the custom to lay before
people nothing in matters of argument but premises, and leave them to
draw conclusions themselves; which, though it could not be done in all
cases, might in many" (Preface, sec. 1, to the *Fifteen Sermons*). Butler would
lay out only premises. The Socratic dialogue does more, drawing conclusions, some of which produce a perplexity. Why the added device of
perplexing? Meno asks the same question of Socrates (80a–b). Socrates'
answer is that there is a further advantage to perplexing. It can undo
the damage done by expositions and aphorisms that have been too poorly
understood. Socrates' description of the slave boy perplexed about ge-
ometry applies as well to those, such as Meno, who are perplexed about
virtue:

> Observe, Meno, the stage he has reached. . . . At the beginning he did not
> know. . . . Nor indeed does he know now, but then he thought he knew
> and answered boldly, as was appropriate—he felt no perplexity. Now how-
> ever he does feel perplexed. Not only does he not know the answer; he
> doesn't even think he knows. . . . We have helped him to some extent to-
> ward finding out the right answer, for now not only is he ignorant of it,
> but he will be quite glad to look for it. (85a–b, trans. Guthrie)

2.3 Conclusion

In the rest of this book, I shall be concerned mainly with arguments that
are not aporetic in their style, neither in themselves nor in the context of
the dialogues of which they are part. But these arguments have, together,
produced aporia in readers by establishing that pleasure is and is not the
good for human beings, and that virtue (hence, apparently, not pleasure)
is the good (see chapter 1). I propose the following interpretive method
for reading Plato, whether in his aporetic or his non-aporetic dialogues.
It is easy to see that a given one-sentence answer is part of an expository
writer's position. But an interpreter cannot say if or in what sense Plato,
the dialogue writer, or the teacher (usually Socrates) within the dialogue
accepts a given one-sentence answer, unless he also understands enough
other parts of Plato's position to be able to tell whether the teacher need
accept or give up that answer along with the student. Given a dialogue, it
is important to try to find an understanding of the teacher's whole position throughout the dialogue. With that whole position, as well as can be

made out, a reader may try to decide whether or not, and in what sense, the teacher holds any given one-sentence answer as part of his position. As Socrates promises Protagoras at the end of the dialogue in his name: "If we could be clear about that, it would throw the fullest light on the question over which you and I have spun such a coil of argument" (360e–361a, trans. Guthrie).

THREE

Ethical Protagoreanism

A t the level of one-sentence answers, there are a number of striking conflicts between the *Gorgias* and the *Protagoras*.[1] (1) At *Gorgias* 495a–d Callicles claims that "pleasure and good are the same." At *Protagoras* 351e5–6 Socrates makes the very same claim. But in the *Gorgias* (500d) Socrates refutes Callicles' position (that is, Socrates' stated position in the *Protagoras*). (2) At *Protagoras* 351c Socrates argues that the good life is one of pleasure while Protagoras suggests that some pleasures are good, some bad; but at *Gorgias* 492c, 494c, 494e, and 497a, Callicles holds that the good life is one of unrestrained pleasure and now it is Socrates who tries to refute it. (3) At *Protagoras* 354a–d Socrates claims that pleasure is the goal that makes good things worthy of pursuit; but at *Gorgias* 506c–d Socrates asserts that pleasure is to be pursued for the sake of the good, not vice versa. On the basis of such evidence it is as easy to see the *Gorgias* as an attack on hedonism as to see the *Protagoras* as a defense of it. Such a reading causes an interpretive dilemma for those who seek to ascribe a coherent ethical theory to Socrates that underlies his argumentation in both dialogues. One solution to this dilemma is to deny that the *Gorgias* attacks hedonism in general. Hence Gosling and Taylor (1982: 69–78), attentive to the coils of argument as well as the concluding one-sentence answers, see Socrates' arguments against Callicles as an attack only on the "life devoted to the satisfaction of short-term bodily appetite" (p. 71)–what they call "short-term" hedonism. In their view, this attack in no way extends to the long-term hedonism that Socrates defends in the *Protagoras*.[2]

Gosling and Taylor are right to deny that the *Gorgias* attacks hedonism in general; they are wrong in the distinction they draw between kinds of hedonism. I argue in this and the following two chapters that the *Gorgias* does not argue against hedonism but against what I shall call *ethical Protagoreanism*.

3.1 Long-term and Short-term Hedonism

The Distinction Between Long-term and
Short-term Hedonism

An example should make clear the distinction between long-term and short-term hedonism. Early in the *Iliad*, Agamemnon announced that he would take Achilles' prize, the fair Briseis, away to his own tent. Homer tells us:

> And pain came to Peleus' son.
> In hairy chest his heart pulled two ways:
> To draw sharp blade from hip, scatter
> The bystanders, then cut Atreus' son down;
> Or else to stop bitterness and hold spirit down.
> (*Il.* I lines 188–192)

Achilles, "pulling the big sword out of the scabbard" (line 194), was about to seek the immediate satisfaction of his bitter spirit. But the goddess Athena comes down from the sky to persuade him to stop and hold down his spirit. She predicts a comparatively greater long-term satisfaction that Achilles will gain.

> Someday gifts three times as splendid
> Shall go to you on account of this outrage.
> (lines 213–214)

In this example divine advice stops and holds down immediate desires, advice that is justified in terms of a greater satisfaction in the long run. Rather than rely on divine advice for enlightenment, Socrates in the *Protagoras* argues that our salvation in life depends on a science of measurement that will allow us to make for ourselves such comparisons with accuracy (356b–357b).

*How the Long-term/Short-term Distinction Reconciles
the Doctrines of the* Protagoras *and* Gorgias

The Gosling and Taylor account has this advantage: it allows us to say
that, although the *Gorgias* does attack the uncalculated, impulsive hedonism of the unenlightened Achilles, nothing in the *Gorgias* is incompatible
with the Socratic measurement craft of hedonism set out in the *Protagoras*.
In particular, the distinction Socrates draws in the *Gorgias* between what
is pleasant and what is good (500d) can be understood in terms of crafty
hedonism as the distinction between what is immediately pleasant and
what is most pleasant overall. According to Gosling and Taylor (1982:
72–73), Socrates' arguments against Callicles show only that one must
distinguish goodness from immediate pleasantness; Socrates' crafty hedonism of the *Protagoras* makes the same distinction. In this way the apparent conflicts between the two dialogues can be reconciled.

Problems with the Long-term/Short-term Distinction

The Gosling and Taylor account escapes from the dilemma facing the
traditional interpretations. But it runs into a problem of its own in the
Protagoras. In order to state this problem, it is necessary to go over part of
Socrates' argument in that dialogue.

3.2 The Argument against *Akrasia*

In the *Protagoras*, Socrates wishes to show that virtue is knowledge (361b1–
2). As part of this task, he attempts to show that whenever a man knows
what is best, he will always choose it. "Now obviously," as Aristotle says,
"this reasoning contradicts what appears to happen" (*NE* VII.2 1145b27–
28). What appears to happen, all too often, is that one's knowledge is
impotent in the grip of anger, desire, fear, or the like. Socrates argues that
such experiences are not in fact cases of impotence (*akrasia*); he argues that
the proper explanation of these experiences is not impotent knowledge
but simple ignorance.

Socrates' argument is a reduction to absurdity. First he establishes a
sentence of the form *P*.

P. A man does (*anthrôpos prattei*) unpleasant things, knowing that they
are unpleasant, because he is overcome by pleasures that are obviously
not a match for [or are obviously exceeded by; see 356a1, *hyperbolê*] the
pains (355e6–356a1).

He completes the proof with a sentence of the form "not-P" (or, as here, "necessarily not-P").[3]

~P. But if the pleasant things are exceeded by the pains, one cannot do (*ou praktea*) them (356b8–c1).

Sentence P follows from the account of *akrasia* ascribed to the many at 355a7–b1 and the interchangeability of the terms *good* and *pleasant* as well as *bad* and *painful*, which is licensed by the ethical hedonism (that is, the doctrine that pleasure is the good) that Socrates establishes. Sentence ~P is one component of the psychological hedonism (that is, the doctrine that one inevitably chooses to do what seems most pleasant) that Socrates establishes and articulates at 356a5–c3.

To prove his point, Socrates needs to hold that there is a single standard by which all choices can be measured. To see how crucial this commensurability claim is, consider the following cases.[4] A wage earner is offered a choice between a 1 percent and a 10 percent pay raise.

1. The wage earner fears that the larger raise will require a longer working day (or a more stressful position in the company, or some such change in his duties).
2. The wage earner believes his duties will remain the same in either case but fears resentment from fellow workers if he accepts the larger raise (or fears that he will feel uncomfortably in debt to his boss, or some such change in his personal relations).
3. The wage earner believes his duties and personal relations will remain the same, but feels unworthy of the larger raise (or feels contempt for excessive financial gain, or is charmed by the novelty of 1 percent, or has a fetish for 1 percent, or has some other such feeling).[5]
4. The wage earner believes a raise is in his own best interest, the larger the better, and (unlike the other cases) finds no strings attached to either choice.

In the first three cases I can imagine how the wage earner may justifiably convince himself that the best thing is to take the larger raise (or smaller—it makes no difference to my point), and let me suppose that his justified belief is true. Still, I might imagine, when the decisive moment comes he is overcome by a desire (to avoid longer work hours or to avoid resentment from fellow workers or to avoid having particular feelings) and chooses the smaller pay raise. Most people say that in these cases "men recognize the best but are unwilling to act on it, . . . overcome by pleasure or pain" (*Prt.* 352d6–e2, trans. Guthrie).

None of these first three cases seems to be a simple more against less; there seems to be no single standard of measurement available to the man making the choice. And this is how it seems "to most people" (*tois pollois anthrôpois*, 352b2–3): "the faculty of knowledge in the man" (*enousês . . . epistêmês*, 352b5–6) "has no basis from which it can lead or rule" (*ouk ischuron oud' hêgemonikon oud' archikon*, 352b4). Without some standard by which to measure one against the other (*atechnôs*; see 352b8), his knowledge like a slave will be pushed around by any impulse (*hôsper peri andrapodou, perielkomenês hupo tôn allôn hapantôn*, 352c1–2).

The fourth case is a simple more against less. Here there is a single standard of measurement, and in this case it is incomprehensible that the desire for the 1 percent should overcome the desire for the 10 percent, unless the man is simply ignorant that 10 percent is larger. Here is one way to see the incomprehensibility: suppose that the man's conscious beliefs and desires are exactly as in case 4, yet while this is so he intentionally chooses the 1 percent. This choice is inexplicable unless I postulate unconscious desires—to be surprising, say, or perverse. And these unconscious desires would destroy the hypothesis of a simple more against less.

What do these cases show? Not before, but as soon as Socrates is granted his hedonist thesis that there is a single standard of pleasure by which all our choices can be measured, his conclusion cannot be resisted that *akrasia* is impossible. For all cases of choice, by that thesis, will be like case 4. It will be impossible for anyone who knows how to measure things by that standard to be overcome by desires to gain pleasures or to avoid pains that by hypothesis are commensurably lesser.[6]

I have demonstrated that if there is a single standard then *akrasia* is impossible. I have not established that there is a single standard ("strong monism," in Stocker's terms). Strong monism is implausible as a doctrine of a hedonism of sense pleasure, for sense pleasures are too varied (this argument against monism is given by Stocker 1990: 218–233). But on other grounds I deny that Socrates' monism is based on sense pleasure hedonism (see chapter 6).

3.3 The Problem for the Long-term/Short-term Interpretation

Now the problem that the *Protagoras* presents for the Gosling and Taylor account may be stated. Gosling and Taylor reconciled the *Gorgias* with the *Protagoras* by claiming that Socrates' hedonism in the *Protagoras* rested on a distinction between immediate and long-term pleasure. But such a hedonism does not seem to allow for a single standard of pleasure. This loss of commensurability can be seen if a fifth case for the wage earner is considered.

5. If the wage earner chooses the smaller raise, he will receive the 1 percent all
    at once, now, as a bonus. If he chooses the larger, he will be paid the 10 per-
    cent (with interest) all at once a year from now.

As in the first three cases, this no longer is a simple case of more against
less. For it is possible to imagine the wage earner justifiably convincing
himself that the larger raise is best yet, overcome by nothing but its immediacy, at the decisive moment choosing the smaller. It is important
that it be only the immediacy which overcomes him. If it is the case that
he is overcome instead by, say, the feel of the cold, hard cash, so that case
5 becomes like case 3, then I have smuggled in an incommensurability
that need not be a result of the distinction between immediate and long-
term pleasure. Of course, usually when a person is accused of being overcome by the "feel" of cash or whatever, nothing more is meant but the
immediacy, which happens to be in tangible form, of the pleasure, not
the feeling as such.

Here, then, is the problem for the Gosling and Taylor account. Socrates,
in trying to establish that knowledge is sufficient for virtuous action,
develops a doctrine of hedonism because he needs commensurability. But
the Gosling and Taylor version of hedonism does not provide for commensurability; it destroys it.[7]

3.4 Real and Apparent Magnitudes of Pleasure in the *Protagoras*

The Distinction Between Real and Apparent Magnitude of Pleasure

The source of the problem for Gosling and Taylor is that they have mistaken the distinction between immediate and long-term pleasures for the
crucial distinction Socrates in fact draws, between real and apparent magnitude of pleasures. In fact Socrates denies that there is any qualitative
difference between immediate and long-term pleasure. "If anyone objects
that there is a great difference between present pleasure and pleasure or
pain in the future, I shall reply that the difference cannot be one of anything else but pleasure and pain" (*Prt.* 356a5–8, trans. Guthrie). Instead,
Socrates' hedonism distinguishes real from apparent magnitudes of one
commensurable pleasure.

So like an expert in weighing, put the pleasures and the pains together,
set both the near and distant in the balance, and say which is the greater

quantity. . . . That being so, answer me this: . . . The same magnitudes seem greater to the eye from near at hand than they do from a distance. This is true of thickness and also of number, and sounds of equal loudness seem greater near at hand than at a distance. If now our happiness consisted in doing, I mean in choosing, greater lengths and avoiding smaller, where would lie salvation? In the art of measurement [which yields real magnitudes] or in the impression made by appearances [which yields only apparent magnitudes]? (*Prt.* 356a8–d4, trans. Guthrie)

How This Distinction Likewise Reconciles the Protagoras and Gorgias

Just as with the immediate/long-term distinction, this real/apparent distinction will reconcile the *Protagoras* and *Gorgias*. Socrates' arguments against Callicles show only that one must distinguish goodness from apparent pleasantness (see chapters 4 and 5). Socrates' hedonism of the *Protagoras*, which distinguishes real from apparent magnitudes of pleasure, makes the same distinction. Thus Socrates' attack against Callicles' position in the *Gorgias* will not extend to the hedonism of measure that Socrates defends in the *Protagoras*.

How This Distinction Supports the Argument in the Protagoras

Socrates' hedonism, which postulated a single standard of pleasure by which all choices in life become—for the possessor of the metric art— like case 4, rules out the possibility of *akrasia*. The problem with the distinction between immediate and long-term pleasure was that it brought on the sort of incommensurability seen in case 5. This incommensurability destroyed Socrates' anti-*akrasia* argument, for most people would claim that a person may have knowledge of long-term pleasure but a stronger desire for immediate pleasure.

Does the distinction between real and apparent magnitude of pleasure likewise destroy Socrates' anti-*akrasia* argument? Will it be plausible to claim that a person may have knowledge of the truly greater magnitude of pleasure but be overcome by a stronger desire for the apparently greater magnitude? To answer, consider another pay-raise case.

6. As in case 4, the wage earner believes a pay raise is in his own best interest, the larger the better, and finds no strings attached to either choice. Whichever he chooses he will receive now, in one lump sum; the two sums are at either end of the table before him. However, the smaller amount is entirely

in one-dollar bills and forms a great big pile, while the larger amount is in one small check.

To elaborate, imagine that the man, faced with this choice, feels a sudden impulse to possess the pile of dollars rather than the check. Perhaps he imagines the delight of spilling open his briefcase at home to surprise his children; perhaps he wants to know how it feels to hug that many dollar bills. In such cases there is no longer a simple more against less. Extraneous desires, to surprise children or feel bundles of bills, that are not a consequence of the distinction between real and apparent magnitude of pleasure have sneaked into the case. Such cases fail to test the distinction to see if it destroys the incommensurability that Socrates needs.

What is needed to test the real/apparent distinction is a case of really more but apparently less without such extraneous desires. But how could that be? I must imagine the wage earner, faced with the two piles, to know that the 10-percent check is a larger amount of money but somehow to have it seem to him that the 1-percent pile is the larger amount of money. I can imagine a man who mistrusts checks. He might choose the pile of dollars, but only because of a qualitative difference: the pile seems certain to him in a way that the check seems uncertain. Here again an extraneous desire has come in: for certainty as well as increase. I can imagine someone childlike, who at the last moment cannot really believe that the little check is worth more than that great big pile; but now of course he does not really know after all that the 10-percent check is a larger amount. I conclude that, in the case of abstract quantities, such as quantities of money, one cannot know that a quantity is greater unless it appears greater.

This conclusion does not seem to hold for concrete quantities. I know that the sun is larger than my hand, yet it can seem smaller. In a more concrete way I can imagine the wage earner being offered both raises in solid gold. Now the table might be arranged so that the nearer looks bigger, though the man knows that in fact the larger amount of gold is at the far end of the table, apparently smaller. Here one may perhaps be able to imagine how the man might choose the apparently bigger, yet somehow know it to be smaller.

But pleasure is abstract in the way that money is but gold is not. Pleasure, if it is like money in being susceptible to a single standard of measurement, will be far more abstract than money in the sense that it can appear with even greater variety and particularity than money. I conclude that with pleasure as much as with money one cannot know that a quantity is greater unless it appears greater. And thus the distinction between real and apparent magnitudes of pleasure, unlike the distinction between pleasures of short and long term, does not destroy Socrates' anti-*akrasia* argument in the *Protagoras*.

3.5 Real and Apparent Magnitudes of Pleasure in the *Gorgias*

Gosling and Taylor saw the Socrates of the *Gorgias* as out to refute only that hedonism which identifies goodness with immediate pleasure. But a more satisfying picture of the *Gorgias* emerges if the crucial distinction Socrates needs there is the same distinction as he drew in the *Protagoras*, between real and apparent magnitudes of pleasure. This and closely related distinctions between the real and the apparent are crucial to Socrates' refutations of both Polus and Callicles.

Polus's Position[8]

Socrates and Polus agree that rhetoric enables one to do "what seems best." Polus believes it follows that rhetoric gives one "great power" and enables a man to do "what he desires." Socrates denies that these follow (466b11–467b9). Their dispute, then, is over the truth of a conditional. Polus believes that if rhetoric enables a man to do what seems best to him, then it enables him to do what he desires. Socrates is "shocking and monstrous" (467b10) to deny it.

Polus's view may be stated as two claims:

1. For any action or object, insofar as it appears to be desirable for me, it really is desirable for me.
2. For any psychological state of mind, insofar as it appears to be a state of desiring, it really is that state of desiring.

Claims 1 and 2 are both species of the more general claim made by the Protagoras of the *Theaetetus*: as things appear to a man, so they really are for him. There Protagoras does not admit any philosophical distinction between the apparent and the real, and he gives a sophisticated epistemological defense of his claim.[9] Thus in the *Gorgias*, although the issue is confined to the level of ethics, pleasure, and desire, the debate is the same as in the *Theaetetus*, where the issue is at a general epistemological level.

Protagoreanism can appear irrefutable when restricted to psychological states such as desire. Polus, with claims 1 and 2, is in strong company. Descartes, for example, accepts the appearance/reality distinction nearly everywhere: he admits that we might be completely deceived about the nature of the world, even about the simplest truths of mathematics (and hence logic). But he denies that this distinction holds for a variety of care-fully delimited psychological states, including desires.[10] To refute Polus's brand of Protagoreanism, Socrates gets him to accept two distinctions, between extrinsic and intrinsic desirables and between conditional and unconditional desiring.

The Distinction between Extrinsic and Intrinsic Desirables

Socrates draws this distinction with a couple of examples (the same distinc-tion is drawn by Brink 1989: 217). The drinking of foul-tasting medicine, which is not desired for its own sake, is opposed to the health for the sake of which we drink. And working for pay is opposed to wealth (467c–d). Here the drinking and working are desirable only extrinsically.[11] Health and wealth, relative to drinking medicine or working for pay, are suggested by Socrates and accepted by Polus as examples of intrinsic desirables. Socrates also has a category of intrinsic undesirables and its correspondent, the ex-trinsic undesirables.[12] It follows from the *Euthydemus*, in which health and wealth are the first two examples of goods mentioned by Socrates (279a), that even these are only contingently good or bad and have no intrinsic value (281b–d). The least controversial example of an intrinsic good, shared by Socrates, Polus, and Callicles, is living well or living happily.

By the way, Aristotle adopts the intrinsic/extrinsic distinction in the first chapter of the *Nicomachean Ethics*. He begins by making the general claim that (to put it in Socrates' terms) every activity is done for the sake of something (1094a1–2). Now someone might object that living well, for instance, is not done for the sake of anything. But Aristotle would reply that such things as living well are done for their own sake. Thus he draws a distinction among the "things for the sake of which," which he calls the "ends" (*tôn telôn*, 1094a3–4). He says that "some ends are the activities [themselves], while others are products apart from the activities" (1094a3–5).[13] When Polus accepts this distinction, Socrates has the premise he needs for his refutation.

The Distinction between Conditional and Unconditional Desiring

With his distinction between intrinsic and extrinsic desirables, Socrates is able to make a further distinction that refutes Polus's Protagoreanism. Socrates lists more examples of things that are possibly extrinsically de-sirable—walking, standing, and for a tyrant, killing, banishing, confiscating. Because they are also possibly extrinsically undesirable, Socrates can claim that we do not desire them unconditionally (468c3). Rather, if these (whatever they are) are "beneficial" (that is, in fact extrinsically desirable), then we desire to do them, and if they turn out to be "harmful" (that is, in fact extrinsically undesirable), then we desire not to do them (468c4–5). Thus we cannot simply say that we desire to kill (or walk or drink medicine), but at best, we conditionally desire these.[14]

By the way, Aristotle does not adopt the conditional/unconditional distinction, but creates another, for he believes that there is a contradiction in Socrates' position. Aristotle offers his own distinction as a solution to the following dilemma. "That desire (*boulêsis*) is for the end has already been stated; to some (i) desire seems to be for the good, while for others (ii) it seems to be for the apparent good" (*NE* III.4 1113a15–16). The first horn is taken by Socrates. According to Aristotle, "It follows that, for the man who chooses incorrectly, what he desires is not desired [by him]" (1113a17–18)—a plain contradiction. Socrates would agree with Aristotle that it follows that what a man chooses incorrectly is not desired by him. Indeed, this consequence is precisely what Socrates will use to refute Polus. But Socrates avoids the plain contradiction of Aristotle by denying that the incorrectly chosen thing is desired in any sense. What Aristotle said about Socrates on *akrasia* seems appropriate here, too: "obviously, this [denial] contradicts what appears to be the case" (*NE* VII.2 1145b27–28).

The second horn is taken by Polus and Callicles. According to Aristotle, "It follows that there is nothing desired by nature" (1113a20–21). Desirability and hence goodness become entirely subjective, which Aristotle cannot accept.

Aristotle's own solution to this dilemma makes the following distinction: "the absolutely (*haplôs*) desirable in truth is the good, but the subjectively (*hekastô(i)*) desirable is the apparent good" (1113a23–24). Aristotle is here distinguishing two senses of the word *desirable*, and claiming that there is a sense (that is, "subjectively") in which we desire the apparent good. This is different from Socrates' distinction. Socrates does not claim that there is any sense in which we desire the apparent good. Instead, he austerely allows us only to assert a pair of conditional sentences: if the apparent good is in fact good, then we desire it; if it is not good, then we do not desire it. This biconditional refutes Polus.

How These Two Distinctions Refute Polus

Socrates has distinguished extrinsic from intrinsic desirability. It follows from this distinction that extrinsic desirability is dependent on causal relations out in the world that may be unknown to the one who desires

(*Grg.* 468d). Therefore (unless I can find a way to be Protagorean about causal relations), I cannot reasonably be Protagorean about extrinsic desirability. The proper explanation, Socrates suggests, is that all my desiring for things I take to be extrinsically desirable is conditional. My abbreviated form of stating a desire, for instance,

I desire to murder

must be understood as biconditional:

I desire to murder if and only if the murder is in fact an extrinsic good for me.

The uncertainty of the right half of this biconditional prevents me from being certain whether I am in a state of desiring. Thus the Protagorean claims 1 and 2 are false, thereby refuting Polus's claim (implicit in Polus's question at *Grg.* 466e3) that if I have the power to do what seems best to me, I have the power to do what I desire. The power of rhetoric or tyranny is not and does not entail the great power that human beings need (*Grg.* 468d7–e3).

Socrates' refutation of Polus is immensely significant to ethics and epistemology.[15] It refutes Polus by showing that the advantages of tyranny or rhetoric are unimpressive in the realm of the extrinsically desirable. But Socrates' refutation is established only in the realm of the extrinsically desirable; hence it is of only limited value in dissuading those who are tempted by the powers of the tyrant and orator. I shall set out this limitation as an objection to Socrates and then argue that Callicles is best understood as taking the very position that is able to make that objection.

The Objection from the Intrinsically Desirable

I will concede that Socrates has refuted Polus regarding the extrinsically desirable. But there remains the intrinsically desirable. Socrates' argument succeeds in the case of the extrinsically desirable because the extrinsically desirable generates only a conditional desire. In contrast, the intrinsically desirable is the result of unconditional desire.

The problem this raises for Socrates in terms of Socrates' own example is clear. According to Socrates, "When we murder . . . we do not unconditionally desire [this act]" (*Grg.* 468c2–3). Socrates has in mind a case, say, where a tyrant has someone killed in order to stay in office. In this case, the murder is part of a rational plan. Accordingly, the murder is desired not for its own sake; the desire is conditional upon beliefs as to the correctness of the plan. Socrates can refute Polus about such desires.

But, I might object, sometimes tyrants desire to murder for its own sake, and not merely because the murder helps produce some overriding end. When desired for its own sake, that is, intrinsically, the murder is unconditionally desired. It is this second case that Socrates' argument against Polus does not affect (this is seen by Penner 1991: 185, n. 30).

It is plausible to maintain that cases where an object becomes intrinsically desirable are not unusual. Among philosophers—to take a case most of us are familiar with—it is not unusual for arguments to be defended only insofar as they seem to lead to truth, professional success, or some other extrinsic goal. But it also sometimes happens that arguments are defended for their own sake, where the defense is made perhaps even in defiance of the truth, chances to enhance professional success, or whatever. The best explanation of such cases is that *to defend* has become intrinsically desirable for the arguer. (Aristotle imagines such an arguer at *NE* I.5 1096a2.) Enough people predictably act on the basis of such desires that the English language has such words as *self-willed, obstinate, stubborn*, and *pertinacious*.

This notion of appetite seems to make it easy for us to know what is intrinsically desirable. For it allows us to restore to Polus a modified version of his two Protagorean claims.

1'. For any action or object, insofar as I feel an appetite for it, it is intrinsically desirable for me.
2'. For any psychological state of mine, insofar as it feels like an appetite to me, it is an unconditional desire of mine.

It is this notion of appetite, and these Protagorean claims, that are found in Callicles' hedonism in the following chapter.

FOUR

Callicles' Hedonism

Callicles claims that the man who is truly "fine and just"—as opposed to the conventionally fine and just—is he who "shall live the right life" (*Grg.* 491e6–8). Such a man "must allow his own appetites to get as big as possible" (*Grg.* 491e8–9). Rather than "restrain" (*kolazein*) them, he must "be endowed by means of manliness and mindfulness (*andreian kai phronêsin*) so as to propel (*hupêretein*)[1] them at their biggest, always to fill up the appetite with its object" (*Grg.* 491e9–492a3).

Callicles shocks conventional wisdom by the rational and ethical egoism implicit in this passage. Rational egoism is a theory of the grounds of reason for action: Callicles believes, evidently, that one has reason to do something just insofar as it promotes one's self-interest. Ethical egoism is a theory of moral obligation: he believes that one has a moral obligation to do something just insofar as it promotes one's self-interest. Both kinds of egoism depend on his theory of self-interest, that is, his answer to the question, What makes one's life go best? His answer is a version of hedonism: one's life goes well just insofar as it is filled with pleasure, which he identifies with the satisfaction of appetite.[2]

So far the interpreters would agree. But there has been no consensus as to what version of hedonist he is, because there are grave difficulties with the versions that have been suggested. These versions may be classified as prudential, indiscriminate, and sybaritic versions of hedonism. In contrast to these, I shall argue that Callicles is best understood as holding a satisfaction hedonism of felt desire with respect to the intrinsically desirable. In what follows, I shall briefly indicate some of the difficulties with the previously suggested alternatives. Then I shall draw the distinctions needed to understand the hedonism I attribute to Callicles and argue for its adequacy.

4.1 The Previous Alternatives

Prudential Hedonism

Prudential hedonists seek to maximize their pleasure in the course of their lives. Such maximization requires one to weigh short-term against long-term considerations of pleasure. This deliberation, often performed in the face of immediate temptations, requires "manliness and mindfulness" (*Grg.* 492a1–2), which are abilities traditionally ascribed to prudence. As an interpretation of Callicles, prudential hedonism has the advantage of being a position worthy of serious philosophical consideration.[3]

A problem with this interpretation is that Socrates' two arguments against Callicles (the argument from opposites, *Grg.* 495e–497d, and the argument from pleased cowards, *Grg.* 497d–499a, both of which I examine in chapter 5) do not address prudential hedonism. The arguments Socrates gives aim to force Callicles to concede that there is a difference between the pleasant and the good. According to the argument from opposites, there is a difference in that the pleasure of appetite satisfaction requires the existence of the pain of appetite, whereas goodness excludes the existence of its opposite. For example, the pleasure of drinking requires the existence of the pain of thirst: when the thirst stops, the pleasure also stops. By contrast, a state of goodness, say in the eyes, excludes the state of badness: for an eye to be healthy it cannot be diseased (at the same time, in the same respect).

Whatever this argument shows, it is obvious that it does not affect prudential hedonism. For the prudential hedonist has no stake in the claim that drinking when thirsty is good, but rather in the claim that *maximizing* experiences such as drinking when thirsty, over the course of a lifetime, is good. And *maximizing* excludes *failing* to maximize every bit as much as health excludes disease. Thus the argument from opposites, if directed against prudential hedonism, is a non-starter.[4]

According to the argument from pleased cowards, there is a difference between the pleasant and the good in that base people, such as cowards, can feel as much pleasure as good (for example, brave) people under certain circumstances. This occurs, for example, in battle, when the enemy withdraws. But their feeling as much pleasure does not make them as good.

Again, this argument does not touch prudential hedonism. For the prudential hedonist has no stake in the claim that brave or good people *on every occasion* are distinguished from the cowardly or base in feeling more pleasure. They claim, rather, that the brave, in the course of a lifetime, will live more pleasantly than the cowardly. This commits the prudential hedonist only to the claim that there are *some* decisive aspects of a brave life in which it is more pleasant than a cowardly life. Thus the argument from pleased cowards, if directed against prudential hedonism, is misguided.[5]

It is particularly embarrassing to attribute to Plato an interpretation that causes these arguments to fail in an obvious way, for the issue with Callicles is of the highest importance for Plato's ethical thought (*Grg.* 487e7–488a2), and these two arguments are the chief weapons he uses to attack Callicles' position. For these reasons I am inclined to look for a better interpretation of Callicles' position than prudential hedonism.

Indiscriminate Hedonism

Whereas prudential hedonists will calculate and sacrifice some of their pleasures in the interests of maximizing their pleasure overall, indiscriminate hedonists follow a policy of satisfying all of their appetites. According to this reading, "it is best to satisfy present desires without restraint" (Irwin 1979: 205; see also Irwin 1977: 121). Such a Callicles would aim at "maximal gratification of appetites, without any distinction as to which appetites are to be gratified" (Kahn 1983: 109; see also Kahn 1996: 245 and Irwin 1995: 105). If Callicles is read this way, at least the second of Socrates' arguments can be interpreted as a success.[6]

Unfortunately, this interpretation achieves its advantage at the price of making Callicles into a straw man. It may be an ideal of Callicles, which even the tyrant and orator fail to achieve, to satisfy *all* appetites (though he never says this; he does reject conventional temperance at *Grg.* 491d-492c, but it does not follow that he makes an omni-satisfactory claim). Moreover, it may be worthwhile for a philosopher to point out that, even were I ideally strong and clever, without temperance some of my appetites would interfere and conflict with others (Aristotle allots seven words to making this point, *NE* I.8 1099a12). It may even be that it is a part of

the point of Socrates' refutation to point out the impossibility of the indiscriminate program.[7] But when these points have been made against
Callicles, there remains the hero he and many human beings remain
tempted by: the figure with the powers of the tyrant or orator. Those who
are attracted by such heroes are not fully addressed by arguments against
indiscriminate hedonism. I take it to be indisputable that in the *Gorgias*
Plato wants to show the error of valuing the powers of the tyrant and orator. A refutation of indiscriminate hedonism, which is in any case of little
philosophical interest, fails to do this. For let us concede that indiscriminate hedonism "was in fact more appealing to ambitious and gifted young
men such as Alcibiades (or Charmides or a younger Critias) than the more
coldly calculating sacrifice of some desires for others in the interest of a
successful career."[8] It remains true that if Plato merely disillusions such
an audience of indiscriminate hedonism, the attractions of the tyrant's or
orator's life will by and large remain, and Plato's dialogue will therefore
fail.[9] For these reasons I am inclined to look for a better interpretation of
Callicles' position than indiscriminate hedonism.

Sybaritic Hedonism

Whereas indiscriminate hedonists follow a policy of satisfying all of their
appetites, sybaritic hedonists cultivate only short-term, bodily appetites.
This interpretation has been defended as enabling us to make Socrates'
two arguments at least qualified successes, hence not embarrassing
failures.[10]

Unfortunately, it shares the disadvantage of the indiscriminate interpretation: Callicles becomes a straw man. The sort of life to which Callicles
invites Socrates—"speaking in the Assembly and practicing rhetoric and
playing the politician" (*Grg.* 500c5–7, trans. Woodhead)—may, I concede, be pursued by some merely for the short-term, bodily pleasures it
would make available. But there remain those who are attracted to the
tyrant's or orator's life for the sake of its long-term or non-bodily pleasures, including those who delight in the sheer exercise of power, or in
the accomplishment of their will, or in the manipulation of others. And
thus it remains true that if Plato merely disillusions his audience of sybaritic hedonism, there will remain considerable attraction to the tyrant's
or orator's life, and Plato's dialogue will therefore fail.[11]

There is an additional defect to the sybaritic interpretation: it is ruled
out by the text. For Callicles subscribes, without being forced by argument, to Socrates' distinction between pleasures of the body and pleasures
of the soul:

Consider then . . . whether you believe that there are certain . . . occupations relating to the soul also—some of them in the nature of arts, exercising forethought for what is best for the soul, others neglecting this but, as in the case of the body, preoccupied entirely with the soul's pleasure, and how it may be achieved—but as to which pleasures are better or worse, this they have never considered, their sole concern being to gratify these pleasures, whether for better or for worse. For I believe, Callicles, that there are such processes,[12] and behavior of this kind I call flattery, *whether it concerns the body or the soul or whatever the object* to whose pleasure it ministers without paying any heed to what is better or worse. Do you subscribe to the same opinion with me, or oppose it? (*Grg.* 501b1–c6, trans. Woodhead, italics mine)

Callicles grudgingly agrees—he says he agrees in order to let Socrates' argument run its course, that Gorgias's appetite (expressed at *Grg.* 497b5) might be satisfied. What he grudges is the separation of pleasure from good, which Socrates has laboriously forced him to accept and especially the consequence that rhetoric is mere flattery; he does not grudge that the soul as well as the body has pleasures and hence appetites. That Callicles does not grudge to apply his notions of appetite and satisfaction to souls as well as bodies is shown by the fact that he ascribes to Gorgias, as shown in this passage, an appetite to hear an argument out—such an appetite is in no way bodily.

There are many other passages which likewise show that Callicles' notion of appetite is not limited to the bodily. If Calliclean appetites were necessarily bodily, Socrates' restriction, "pleasures *of the body*" (*Grg.* 499d4–5) would have no point. Again, the lack of discipline, and hence the appetites (referred to at *Grg.* 507c–508c) are plainly meant to extend beyond the bodily. And Callicles speaks of a tyrant "wishing" to put a man to death (*Grg.* 511a); presumably he would have no scruples about describing such a man as having a non-bodily appetite to kill. Moreover, citizens are described as having an appetite for ships, walls, dockyards, revenues, harbors, and the like (*Grg.* 518e3 with 517c2–3 and 519a2–3): such appetites are impossible to construe as bodily. Also, most people "find pleasure in" honors (*Grg.* 526d5–6): such a satisfaction is not of a bodily appetite. Indeed, the italicized words "or whatever the object" (*Grg.* 501c3–4) in the passage I have quoted at length above show that neither Socrates nor Callicles necessarily would restrict appetites only to body and soul; it is left open that there may be other subjects of appetite. So the text does not let us restrict Callicles' notion of appetite to the bodily.

Nor is it a plausible reading of the text to restrict Calliclean appetites to the short term. Just as Gorgias may have an appetite to hear out a lengthy argument, a Calliclean hero may have an appetite to have any number of long-range plans put into effect, as many of the examples in the preceding paragraph show. Indeed an appetite to live *a life*[13] of power, honor, and wealth can safely be ascribed to Callicles. Such appetites are not short term.

Consequently, because it makes Callicles' position a straw man, and because of textual infidelity, I am inclined to look for a better interpretation of Callicles' position than sybaritic hedonism.

4.2 Other Classifications of Hedonism

All hedonist theories of self-interest share the doctrine that goodness in a life consists in pleasure. But there are different accounts of what should be considered as pleasure. A number of classifications of hedonism have been explored since the turn of the century, several of which it will be useful to set out here, together with some brief consideration of their relative merits, and an attempt to locate Callicles as far as possible among them.

Stimulation and Satisfaction

Is pleasure essentially a matter only of stimulation or only of satisfaction, or may it be either?[14] *Stimulation* hedonism restricts pleasure and pain to experience with a distinctive qualitative feeling. I suppose it is easiest to understand in its materialist form—call it *C-fiber* hedonism—which would attempt to identify pleasure with the stimulation of certain fibers in the nervous system or brain. But stimulation hedonism proper is a purely phenomenal claim: pleasure, like pain, consists in the sensation of a specific type of feeling. This view is usually, and rightly, judged to be too narrow to capture the wide range of experiences human beings find pleasure in. Consider, as Parfit (1984: 493) says, "the pleasures of satisfying an intense thirst or lust, listening to music, solving an intellectual problem, reading a tragedy, and knowing that one's child is happy." These experiences do not appear to share any common phenomenological stimulation (see also Goldstein 1985 and Griffin 1986: 8–9).

As has already been shown in the discussion of sybaritic hedonism, Callicles as much as Parfit is aware of the wide range of experiences human beings take pleasure in: eating and drinking, hearing arguments, having an enemy put to death, and possessing ships or honors. So Callicles is certainly not a narrow stimulation hedonist. In fact he explicitly restricts pleasure not to stimulation but to the satisfaction of appetite: "there is no longer any pleasure for the man who is satisfied" (*Grg.* 494a6–7).[15] And since, as has been shown, Callicles' use of the term *appetite* (*epithumia*) cannot be restricted to the bodily or short-term appetites, the term *appetite*, as used by Callicles, should connote no narrower a range of application than *desire* or *preference*, though *appetite* perhaps suggests a greater intensity of feeling.

Satisfaction hedonism restricts pleasure to the satisfaction of desire: this is clearly Callicles' hedonism. Such an account appears to capture a wide range of pleasures. Nonetheless, like the stimulation theory, it may seem too narrow. For there are pleasures of sense perception unrelated to satisfaction. Dent (1984: 39), developing an example that goes back to Plato's *Republic* (584b), points out that pleasures of smell, such as the fragrance of a rose, do not require an antecedent desire for rose scent or even for scent in order to be pleasant. The point can be made with any of the five senses:

> Why one degree of pressure in the rubbing of the skin is appropriate
> to cause a pleasurable experience, whereas others do not (but hurt or
> tickle), . . . does not at all derive from the agent's prior desire to have just
> the experience that that degree of pressure produces. (Dent 1984: 40–41)

The consideration of such pleasures of sense perception might drive us to a *disjunctive* theory of pleasure as either satisfaction or stimulation. A disjunctive theory undoubtedly conforms more closely to the ordinary uses of the words *pleasure* and *pain* (and their Greek equivalents, as *Rep.* IX 584b shows) than the theories of pleasure as exclusively stimulation or exclusively satisfaction.

Despite this consideration, Callicles is right to ignore the occurrence of non-satisfying but pleasant stimulations in his concern with hedonism as an account of self-interest, and may even be right in attempting a revision of our ordinary uses of the words *pleasure* and *pain*, though it is possible to quibble with him about usage. Let us look more carefully at the pleasures and pains of sense perception to see why.

Dent's example of massage shows, I think, that a desire for a particular degree of pressure is not the reason why that particular stimulation is pleasant. But it does not show that the reason for the pleasure is intrinsic to the particular feeling of that stimulation. Indeed the raw feel of the stimulation cannot be the reason why the stimulation is pleasant or painful. For, "after taking certain kinds of drug, people claim that the quality of their sensations has not altered, but they no longer dislike these sensations. We would regard such drugs as effective analgesics" (Parfit 1984:

501). Likewise there are states of depression where the rose smells or the massage feels the same as ever, yet these very sensations no longer are pleasant. And the understanding can play a role in mitigating or enhancing the pleasure or pain of a sensation (see section 7.4 of this book).

Moreover, only satisfaction, not stimulation, has significance for self-interest. A case where stimulation and satisfaction diverge in a striking way can be found in Freud's life. Near death, "Freud refused pain-killing drugs, preferring to think in torment than to be confusedly euphoric" (Griffin 1986: 8, citing Jones 1964: 655–656; see also Parfit 1984: 494). In an ordinary way of speaking, Freud had reason to prefer pain. But I do not think it nonsense to describe him in this case as finding the feeling of what we ordinarily call "pain" less miserable, or even less painful, than euphoric haze. To take a similar case having to do with pleasure instead of pain, consider an ascetic who in meditation might well find the fragrant scent of a rose or the pressure of a massage—the very stimuli that are "pleasant" according to the ordinary usage—to be irritating distractions. Again, I do not think it nonsense to describe such a person as finding the feeling that we in ordinary cases call "pleasure" to be less blessed, or even less pleasant, than the stillness of meditation.

One who insists on narrowly describing these sorts of cases as cases where it is rational to choose pain or not to choose pleasure (rather than as cases where "pain" is less painful than euphoria, or stillness more pleasant than "pleasure") will see them as refutations of hedonism as an account of self-interest, though they leave untouched a desire-satisfaction theory of self-interest. Such insistence will not refute Callicles as a desire-satisfaction theorist. It will only show he is wrong to think of desire satisfaction as the sole nature of pleasure. I have no interest in quibbling over labels; I am happy to give Callicles his revised usage of the words *pleasure* and *pain* and to continue to endorse the interpretative tradition that sees him as a hedonist. But it would not substantially affect my classification of Callicles to see him, henceforth, not as a hedonist but as a desire-satisfaction theorist. However the quibble about word usage is decided, satisfaction will be preferable to stimulation or to a disjunction of either as the correct account of self-interest.

Not only does Callicles identify pleasure with satisfaction; he identifies pain with desire. Filled up, a man is "neither enjoying nor suffering" (*Grg.* 494b1). Moreover, in his model, "every lack—that is [*kai*], appetite—is painful" (*Grg.* 496d4).[16] Once again, Callicles' model is at variance with our ordinary use of the terms *pain* and *desire*:

> Not all cases of hunger, thirst, or sexual desire are unpleasant; one works
> up a nice appetite for lunch, and may find a state of sexual arousal itself

something pleasant. Such appetites are unpleasant not as a general rule, but only when their satisfaction is impossible or excessively delayed.[17]

It seems to me that this criticism fails to show any significant error in Callicles' account. He can continue to maintain that appetites are by their nature unpleasant, since the counter-examples can be explained away. For Callicles can plausibly argue that the examples used in this criticism, which are drawn from cases where the satisfaction of appetite is likely or imminent, depend on a confusion of the pain of appetite with the pleasures of anticipation or titillation. Once the pleasure components have been recognized, the appetite is seen to be in itself painful.

To see that this is so, consider in more detail one of the examples of the objection: suppose that I have completed four hours of a day-long hike in the wilderness. I have now worked up a nice appetite for lunch. I open my pack, only to discover that by oversight I have left my lunch behind, and with it every prospect for a meal. I take it that at the moment of recognition the nice appetite becomes a tiresome burden. The only factor that has changed is that the prospect of the satisfaction of my appetite has become excessively delayed. Thus Callicles can maintain that "nice" appetites are in themselves painful, though the prospects of satisfaction can disguise this pain.

This reply I have made on behalf of Callicles postulates a confusion of anticipatory pleasure with appetite. But against this reply one might object that the reply itself confuses anticipatory pain with appetite: if my four-hour appetite seemed pleasant only because of its apparently imminent satisfaction, my four-hour-and-ten-minute appetite seems painful only because of its impossible or excessively delayed satisfaction.[18] But this objection fails, too. The counter-examples of hunger, thirst, and sexual desire seem pleasant *only* when linked with anticipatory pleasures; if they seemed painful *only* when imagined with anticipatory pains, this objection would have force. But appetites need not be imagined together with anticipatory pains to seem painful: when I abstract from the anticipation of future satisfaction or dissatisfaction, an appetite, insofar as it is felt, is painful. Were this not so, the anticipation of impossible or excessively delayed satisfactions, which is often the anticipation of continued appetite, would not be a pain.

It might seem that cases of sexual desire are different. For sexual arousal, in itself, can be pleasant in a way that hunger and thirst seem not to be.[19] But I maintain that Callicles' account is as true of sexual desire as of hunger and thirst. For a distinction needs to be drawn between sexual desire and titillation. Titillation is not painful, but neither is it an appetite. To see the distinction, consider the parallel in cases of hunger and thirst.

Advertisements for food and drink of a particularly glossy and sophisti-cated kind can provide a pleasure that is not anticipatory of eating and drinking yet is associated with those pleasures. Though the pain of hun-ger and the pleasure of anticipation may heighten and be heightened by these gustatory titillations, the hunger and the titillations are not the same. In a parallel manner, felt sexual appetite is different from titillations as well as anticipations. And felt sexual appetite, when conceived apart from the two subsidiary pleasures of titillation and anticipation, may be plau-sibly seen as in itself painful.

I do not think that it is oversubtle to see Callicles as one who recog-nizes that there can be pleasures (such as anticipatory and titillative) in managing the pains which are appetites. Such management may be part of the program of cultivation of appetite which he recommends: a man "must allow his own appetites to get as big as possible" (*Grg.* 491e8–9). Rather than "restrain them," he must "be endowed by means of manli-ness and mindfulness so as to propel them at their biggest, always to fill up the appetite with its object" (*Grg.* 491e9–492a3). The true Calliclean hero would not, of course, have forgotten his food as in the above hiking scenario. But had he been put in a situation like that, if he were "manly" enough to walk through the day without food, and "mindful" enough to cultivate such an appetite with the assurance that he would be able to "propel" it at its largest so as finally to fill it up with its object, then it might be expected of him to actually enjoy, as he walks, not the pain which is that appetite, but the prospect of a heroic satisfaction. Because the pros-pect of satisfaction is closely connected to the experience of the pain, it could be said that such a hero "enjoys" a ferociously "nice" appetite, but the fact remains that felt appetites in themselves are painful. I conclude, then, that Callicles' account of pain as desire plausibly captures what is significant about both for self-interest.

Counterfactual Satisfaction

Should satisfaction hedonism attach value only to the satisfaction of the appetites or preferences that someone actually has? Suppose that I spend my afternoon nibbling snacks every half hour. I never actually get the big appetite for supper that I would otherwise have. Since I do not actually hunger for a large meal, I could not be faulted by a satisfaction hedonism that takes into account only actual desires. But Callicles clearly would fault me. He recommends the cultivation of the largest appetites possible (*Grg.* 491e8–9). Let me not take up the question at what point, if any, the pain of cultivating a larger appetite begins to outweigh the pleasure of its sat-isfaction. I will even grant, because the point does not strike me as important, that largest might not always be best. Where Callicles clearly is right is in his recognition of the need, in Parfit's words (1984: 496), "to appeal not only to my actual preferences, in the alternative I choose, but also to the [counterfactual] preferences that I would have had if I had chosen otherwise."

Cognitively Counterfactual Satisfaction

There are different ranges of counterfactual affairs that one might consider significant to self-interest. Should satisfaction hedonism consider only the alternatives that directly change my *affective* states, such as, in the example given above, fasting or nibbling through an afternoon? Or should it also consider alternatives that directly change my *cognitive* states? These are the merely possible alternatives in which I possess factual information I actually lack, in which I do not make errors in logical reasoning, and in which I possess concepts adequate to understand the alternatives. Factual information affects desires such as, to take a Socratic example (*Grg.* 468d), when a tyrant wishes to execute a person who seems and is believed to be a threat but who in fact is necessary for the tyrant's preservation. Logical reasoning affects desires by informing us which desires are mutually consistent, helping us adapt means to ends, and freeing us of fallacious considerations. Conceptual ability affects desires by enabling us, in Sidgwick's words (1907: 111–112) "adequately to realise in imagination" the nature and consequences of our choices. An adequate realization in one's imagination that an action is unkind, unfair, or base, for example, often affects the desire to perform it.

A *cognitively actual* satisfaction hedonism asserts that one's good consists in the satisfaction of the desires one may have on the basis of one's actual beliefs about the facts, as well as one's actual logical and conceptual ability. (Note that such a hedonism can consistently be affectively counterfactual.) A *cognitively counterfactual* satisfaction hedonism asserts that one's good consists in the satisfaction of the desires one would have were one to be cognitively *enlightened*, that is, to have complete and accurate factual information and adequate logical and conceptual ability.

The Intrinsically and Extrinsically Desirable

A satisfaction hedonist might draw the cognitively actual/counterfactual distinction with respect to either the intrinsically or extrinsically desirable. As in section 3.5, something is *intrinsically* desirable if it is desirable in or for itself; *extrinsically* desirable if it is desirable as a means to produce, constitute, or in some other way realize something else. For example, a foul-tasting medicine may be only extrinsically desirable to the person for whom it is prescribed. A leisure activity, such as playing golf, may be intrinsically desirable. And a leisure activity that has been prescribed for one's health may be both intrinsically and extrinsically desirable.

The cognitively actual/counterfactual distinction is familiar in our century. Drawn by Sidgwick (1907: 111–112), it has been observed by such recent writers as Parfit (1984: 500–501), Griffin (1986: 12–13), and Brink (1989: 68–69 and 228–230). Yet, as all the authors just cited recognize, there are problems with either a cognitively actual or counterfactual satisfaction theory.

The Problem with a Cognitively Actual Satisfaction Theory

According to the cognitively actual satisfaction theory, the good for me should be what satisfies the desires I may have, given my actual cognitive state. The problem, as Griffin (for example) points out, is that "notoriously, we mistake our own interests. It is depressingly common that when even some of our strongest and most central desires are fulfilled, we are no better, even worse, off" (1986: 10). This sort of mistake is a common theme in literature, for example, in studies of marriages that fail.[20]

The Problem with the Cognitively Counterfactual Satisfaction Theory

According to the cognitively counterfactual satisfaction theory, the good for me should be what satisfies the desires I may have in an enlightened cognitive state. Griffin points out the problem.

> It is doubtless true that if I fully appreciated the nature of all possible objects of desire, I should change much of what I wanted. But if I do not go through that daunting improvement, yet the objects of my potentially perfected desires are given to me, I might well not be glad to have them; the education, after all, may be necessary for my getting anything out of them. That is true, for instance, of acquired tastes; you would do me no favour by giving me caviar now, unless it is part of some well-conceived training for my palate. (1986: 11)

The problem is that sometimes it does no good to gain what would satisfy desires I do not as a matter of fact have, even if I should have them in other circumstances.

There is a further problem. Even when it does me good to have counter-factual desires satisfied, as when some unanticipated and undesired event brings about unexpected happiness, *why* does it? The counterfactual theory seems unable to provide an explanation. Why should it be good for me that desires that do not actually exist are satisfied?[21] Of course, if I have an actual desire for unexpected happiness, there is an explanation of the undesired event's goodness in its contribution to attaining the desired object. But there are people who evidently do not desire unexpected happiness, who yet may find it to be good.[22]

As has just been shown, neither the cognitively counterfactual nor actual theory of self-interest is satisfactory. This failure should lead desire-satisfaction theorists to question the distinction altogether. For my pur-poses there is a reason, both philosophical and exegetical, to reject this distinction.

The Problem with the Cognitively Counterfactual / Actual Distinction

The distinction between the satisfaction of cognitively counterfactual and actual desire is not true to the nature of desire. For it is unable to make sense of the experience of coming to appreciate what one's desires really are. This experience is widespread enough to have provided a familiar device in literature: two characters are portrayed as falling in love in such a way that the reader perceives their mutual desires before the characters do.[23] Coming to appreciate one's true desires is also an experience famil-iar in philosophical investigation. One recent work, for example, begins with this claim:

> By the end of this book, if not before, you may come to have a fuller appre-ciation of some of your central beliefs about yourself, and some of your related attitudes. In particular, you may come to realize more fully that, even as you yourself most deeply believe, after several more decades at most, you will cease to exist, completely and forever. (Unger 1990: 3)[24]

Unger indeed devotes the last chapter of his book to a task he calls "the appreciation of our actual values:" "coming to understand more clearly what our own main values actually are" (1990: 295).

Even more striking than Unger is Socrates in the *Gorgias*. Despite the manifest prestige of successful orators in a city, Socrates claims that they are not esteemed at all by people (*Grg.* 466b3); despite Polus's insistent denial, Socrates claims that not just Polus but indeed all human beings agree with Socrates (*Grg.* 474a5–10); and according to Socrates, if Callicles does not refute Socrates, Callicles will be not merely wrong but in contradiction with himself (*Grg.* 482a6–c3).[25]

To a remarkable extent, Unger and Socrates correctly predict our experience: sometimes we do find ourselves; we do not simply change our minds as a result of thinking through philosophical arguments. Consider, then, the real desires that we sometimes find. Are they cognitively counterfactual or actual desires? Not counterfactual, since we had them all along, both before and after the cognitive enlightenment. But not "actual," according to the twentieth-century distinction, since those are meant to be the desires we recognize prior to cognitive enlightenment. The distinction of desire into actual and counterfactual does not allow us to make sense of this recognition. Thus in drawing this distinction we are unable either to give a correct account of desire or to understand Socrates' claims in the *Gorgias* (such as, as seen above, at 466b3, 474a5–b10 and 482a6–c3).

Nonetheless, the distinction between cognitively counterfactual and actual desire is an approximation to the distinction that will help us characterize Callicles' position: a distinction between the satisfaction of true and felt desire. Before characterizing that distinction between kinds of *desire*, a distinction unfamiliar to, though approximated by, modern theorists, let me, to avoid confusion, point out a different distinction, one which is familiar to modern theorists, between true and felt *satisfaction*.

True and Felt Satisfaction Hedonism

Felt satisfaction hedonism asserts that goodness in a life consists in the psychologically introspected feeling of satisfaction. This account, like stimulation hedonism, restricts ultimate value in a life, implausibly, to a mental state. The problem is we do seem to value things other than states of mind, even independently of the states of mind they produce. Nozick's (1974: 42–45) famous experience-inducing machine, as well as Nagel's (1979) discussion of life insurance make this point (see also Parfit 1984: 494–495; Griffin 1986: 9–10, 14; and Unger 1990: 298–302). Thus *true satisfaction* hedonism is preferable. It asserts that goodness resides in the true satisfaction of one's desires, that is, the sort of satisfaction required of clauses in contracts, a satisfaction not necessarily connected to one's awareness of it.

As I said, I raise this distinction only to separate it from the one I am interested in, between true and felt desire. I do not see the distinction between true and felt satisfactions raised in the *Gorgias*. Though I am inclined to attribute a felt satisfaction hedonism to Callicles (and a true satisfaction thesis to Socrates), I see little in what he says that requires him to hold it. But it is otherwise with hedonism of felt desire.

Hedonism of Felt and True Desire

Hedonism of *felt desire* asserts that goodness consists in the satisfaction of the desires I may believe or feel myself to have; hedonism of *true desire* asserts that goodness consists in the satisfaction of the desires I really have. The distinction is comparable to that between cognitively actual and counterfactual satisfaction. The difference can be seen by adopting the (counterfactual) point of view of myself, after I am cognitively enlightened with the correct information and adequate reasoning and conceptual ability. The question is, How do I describe my change to this enlightened state? Let $B1$ and $B2$ be beliefs and $D1$ and $D2$ be desires. According to the cognitively counterfactual theorist, I ought to say:

When I believed $B1$ I had desire $D1;$ now that I know $B2$ I have desire $D2$.

But according to the theorist of true desire, I ought to say:

$D2$ is the desire I have always had!—I only thought I had desire $D1$ before, when I believed $B1$.

As shown, the true desire theorist, unlike the counterfactual desire theorist, is able to explain the experience of coming to appreciate one's true desires. This difference makes the true/felt distinction preferable to the counterfactual/actual, as it has been understood in this century. Strictly speaking, of course, theorists of both true and felt desire are cognitive actualists. But the true desire theorist can solve the problem for cognitive actualism—what Griffin above called cases of "mistaking our own interest"—without recourse to counterfactual states.

4.3 Socrates' Disagreement with Polus and Callicles

The true/felt distinction allows us to characterize Socrates' disagreements with both Polus and Callicles. Both the success and the limits of Socrates' refutation of Polus have been discussed in chapter 3.

Socrates and Polus Disagree over Whether Desires Are True or Felt with Respect to the Extrinsically Desirable

The root of their disagreement can be seen by an examination of Socrates' first refutation of Polus. Polus was refuted as a result of a Socratic distinction between *conditional* and *unconditional* desire. Extrinsically desirable objects—such things as walking, taking medicine, and for a tyrant, killing, banishing, and confiscating—are not desired "unconditionally" (*haplôs*, 468c3). "Rather, whenever these are advantageous [that is, whenever these in fact realize what is unconditionally desired], we desire to do them, and whenever harmful [that is, they turn out to realize what is unconditionally undesirable], we desire *not* to do them" (*Grg.* 468c3–5).

Notice that Socrates' conditional, just quoted, is not contrary to fact (it is present general); he is not offering a counterfactual desire theory. Instead, Socrates' questions point out *why* a desire can be incompletely understood; hence why there can be true apart from felt desire.

I Postulate that Calliclean Appetite for an Object Makes It Intrinsically Desirable

When Callicles argues that the good life—the life available to orators and tyrants—is one in which I satisfy my appetites at their largest, it need not be assumed that he is merely remaking Polus's mistake, and needing to be shown once again that getting what seems best need not get me what I really want, since the tyrant can be wrong (for example) that killing the prime minister will safeguard the tyranny. That would make for tiresome reading. Instead, it can be understood that Callicles is making a new point, cognizant of the refutation of Polus: whereas for Socrates nothing but knowledge can, at last, be conceived as the intrinsic good (as shown at *Euthyd.* 278e–281e: hence the overriding importance of philosophy), Callicles is claiming, with great apparent plausibility, that almost anything, conceivably, can become an intrinsic good for me. As shown in chapter 3, sometimes tyrants desire to murder for its own sake—intrinsically—and not because the murder helps produce some overriding extrinsic end.

Callicles' notion of appetite can be interpreted to be the faculty in a human being that makes something intrinsically desirable.[26] Callicles' paradigms of appetite—hunger and thirst—are faculties that appear to make eating and drinking intrinsically desirable. Of course, Calliclean appetite, and what may become intrinsically desirable, are not limited to the bodily. If I am an orator or tyrant, such intrinsically desirable objects will be most available to me, while, if I am a Socratic philosopher, they will be least available. Thus, by taking Callicles to be making such a point, his position can still have great force after Polus's defeat. Moreover, given the force of the objection from the intrinsically desirable, it is philosophically necessary for Plato to consider it, if he is to dissuade us from the attractions of tyranny and rhetoric. It has been shown, thanks to Socrates' refutation of Polus, that there is a difference between true and felt desire with respect to the extrinsically desirable, and that my good consists in satisfying my true, not felt, desires for such objects. Can a corresponding distinction between true and felt desire be sensibly drawn with respect to the intrinsically desirable?

Cognitively Counterfactual and Actual Desire for Intrinsically Desirable Objects

Contemporary philosophers have drawn such a distinction between cognitively counterfactual and actual desire. Suppose, in Griffin's words (1986: 12), that "I develop one set of material desires not realizing that they are the sort that, once satisfied, are replaced by another set that are just as clamorous and I am no better off. The consumer desires at the centre of the economists' stage can be like that." Griffin is supposing that, were I to be in the cognitively enlightened state of realizing that consumer desires do not make one's life go better by being satisfied, I might lose those desires and feel others.

These consumer desires can make their objects intrinsically desirable. For example, I might want a luxury car of a particular make, say a BMW, not for status, not for transportation, but just because it is a BMW. The satisfaction theory of cognitively *counterfactual* desire with respect to intrinsically desirable objects would assert that the good for me consists in the satisfaction of the desires I would have in an enlightened state; a satisfaction theory of cognitively *actual* desire would assert that the good for me consists, in Griffin's case, in satisfying my consumer desires.

The cognitively counterfactual/actual distinction faces the same sorts of problems in the special case of intrinsically desirable objects as it does in general. It does not seem best for me to satisfy my consumer desires if I have them only because of my ignorance. But it is hard to see much value in my coming to have what I would, if enlightened, desire (the life of Socrates, let us suppose) if all I can see in that life, given my actual ignorance, is its material poverty. Moreover, even if that alternative (Socratic) life were to have value for me, it is hard to see *why* it should, on any satisfaction theory; for it satisfies, by hypothesis, no desires I actually have.

True and Felt Desire with Respect to the Intrinsically Desirable

Notice that the sort of experience that I described above, the experience of coming to appreciate one's true desires, can occur in the special case of the intrinsically desirable just as they do in general. Indeed the examples

I have already given—in popular literature, of recognizing that one has been in love, and in philosophy, of coming to appreciate one's true values—are easily understood as concerning intrinsically desirable objects. The fact, as has been discussed, that a counterfactual/actual distinction cannot account for this experience is reason to prefer, in the special case of the intrinsically desirable as well as in the general case, the true/felt distinction.

I Postulate that Socrates and Callicles Disagree over Whether Desires Are True or Felt with Respect to the Intrinsically Desirable

It is crucial, in order for Callicles to carry on his praise of the orator's life after the defeat of Polus, that the appetites he encourages us to cultivate be felt appetites; true appetites require expertise to know, an expertise that a tyrant per se does not have. Felt appetites require no expertise; any tyrant knows them. And it is crucial that the appetite be for intrinsically desirable objects; for insofar as the appetite is for extrinsically desirable objects Callicles will be vulnerable to the argument that defeated Polus. Moreover, Socrates cannot, nor does he ever try, to disprove that the life of the orator or tyrant can be full of the satisfaction of felt desire. What he can and does do, though, is to show that Calliclean satisfaction does not give us what is intrinsically desirable (for this argument, see chapter 5 of this book).

Is It True to the Text to Understand Callicles as a Hedonist of Felt Appetite?

Of course Callicles would not describe his notion of appetite in terms of the true/felt distinction, which he does not recognize. It is easy for Callicles to ignore true appetites. Just as Polus initially confused what one desires with what seems best, that is, true and felt desire for the extrinsically desirable, it can be imagined that Callicles has no sense of a true/felt distinction about the intrinsically desirable. Notice that the example from Griffin of consumer desires, which I used to draw the distinction between counterfactual and actual or between true and felt, would not convince Callicles. Socrates' metaphors of the soul as a "leaky jar" (*Grg.* 493b2–3), "sieve" (*Grg.* 493b7), and excremental bird (*Grg.* 494a6) accurately show the problem with consumer desires, yet they do not convince Callicles that such desire is spurious or vain. His reply to these metaphors is that "when the soul is full, there is neither pleasure nor pain. The pleasant life, rather, consists in the largest, most continuous possible influx" (*Grg.* 494a8–b2).

Moreover, Callicles can give a pragmatic justification for neglecting the true: even supposing that there are true appetites, Callicles might plausibly argue that we find them relevant only insofar as they are felt.[27]

The Power and Appeal of Callicles' Position

A myth that effectively shows the power of the position I attribute to Callicles is the ring of Gyges (*Rep.* II 359c–360d): the ring, with its power to confer invisibility, makes it easy to figure out how to get nearly anything one wants. Thus the myth—like the character types of the *Gorgias*, the orator and the tyrant—is a device that abstracts from means-ends considerations, that is, questions of what is extrinsically desirable. Thus the myth sharpens the issue concerning what is intrinsically desirable: would a person with such power be *mistaken* in satisfying any felt desire? Does the satisfaction of felt desires realize the intrinsically desirable? There is a widespread philosophical tradition of great cultural influence that says such people would not, indeed could not, be mistaken in their ultimate desires, and in such satisfactions would, indeed must, realize what for them is intrinsically desirable. That tradition has flourished in philosophers as diverse and influential as David Hume, Max Weber, and Karl Popper.[28] That tradition has arguably shaped Western culture since at least the Renaissance.[29]

4.4 Conclusion: The Calliclean Hedonist Equation

The defining characteristic of Callicles' notion of appetite is not short-term or bodily desire but felt desire for something for its own sake. As has been shown, it is only with such a notion that Callicles' position can have any force after Polus's defeat, and it is only by considering such a notion that Plato can complete his refutation of ethical Protagoreanism.

Thus at issue between Socrates and Callicles are the modified but still Protagorean claims that were discussed in section 3.5:

1'. For any action or object, insofar as I feel an appetite for it, it is intrinsically desirable for me.
2'. For any psychological state of mine, insofar as it feels like an appetite to me, it is an unconditional desire of mine.

Since Callicles wants to identify unconditional desire with appetite, he must claim that they have the same objects. These objects are the intrinsically desirable and the satisfying of appetite. Now Socrates' term for the intrinsically desirable is "the good" (see section 3.5, note 12). And, according to Callicles, the pleasant is nothing but the satisfying of appetite, which in his model is the filling of a lack: "there is no longer any pleasure for the man who is filled up" (494a6–7). Thus Callicles is committed to the identity thesis that, in terms of the text, the good is none other than the pleasant, that is, the intrinsically desirable is none other than the satisfying of appetite. It is this same identity thesis that Socrates' two arguments explicitly refute (497a4–5 with d5–8 and 499a7–d1), as will be demonstrated in the next chapter.

FIVE

Callicles Refuted

A perennial problem for moral theorists is the challenge of immoralism. Plato, through the character of Callicles, gives a classic statement of the immoralist challenge in the *Gorgias* (483b–484c). In addition to Callicles' rational and ethical egoism (see chapter 4), which Socrates does not challenge, Callicles' view is characterized by the hedonist thesis that there is nothing of intrinsic value but the experience of satisfying felt appetites: the larger and more intense the appetite, the greater the value of its satisfaction (491e6–492a3). As demonstrated in chapters 3 and 4, such a hedonism is not the same as the hedonism Socrates apparently defends in the *Protagoras*, nor should it be identified with prudential, indiscriminate, or sybaritic versions of hedonism. It is of the highest importance to Plato to refute Callicles' hedonist thesis (see 487e7–488a2), and for the purposes of such a refutation, he gives two arguments, which I call the argument from opposites (495e–497d) and the argument from pleased cowards (497d–499a). My disagreements with the major recent interpretations of these arguments will be apparent in what follows. But my purpose here is not just explication but defense, for it is my thesis that both arguments are philosophically defensible in their own right.[1]

5.1 The Argument from Opposites

Socrates' first argument refutes Callicles' identity thesis by finding a relation that holds between the intrinsically desirable ("the good") and its
opposite ("the bad"), but which does not hold between the satisfying of
an appetite ("pleasure") and the appetite itself ("pain"). The relation is
that of being held and released "in turn" (496b6–7), which, as Socrates'
discussion shows, is the relation of being mutually exclusive and jointly
exhaustive in a subject:

> If these things [the good and the bad] are opposites, the same must hold
> true of them as of health and sickness. A man cannot be both in health and
> sick at the same time [that is, they are mutually exclusive in a subject],
> nor be rid of both conditions at the same time [that is, they are jointly
> exhaustive in a subject]. (495e6–9, trans. Woodhead)

The condition of joint exhaustion needs clarification. The problem is
that this condition appears to contradict the concession that Socrates drew
from Polus earlier, that in addition to good and bad things there are "in-
between" things that are "neither good nor bad" (467e2).[2] It would appear that, if a subject reaches an in-between condition, her condition will
be neither good nor bad, and hence the subject will, contrary to Socrates'
later claim, be rid of both opposites at the same time.

Must Socrates be interpreted to claim joint exhaustion?[3] Consider for
a moment only his claim that a subject "is not at the same time rid" (*oude
hama apallattetai*) of both health and sickness (495e5–9). "Riddance" in
this passage might perhaps mean either *being* rid of both or merely *becom-
ing* rid of both. If Socrates is claiming that a subject cannot simultaneously
be rid of both, then he is claiming that both are jointly exhaustive in the
subject: the subject must be in one or the other condition, health or sickness. But if Socrates is claiming merely that a subject cannot simultaneously *become* rid of both, he is making a weaker claim than joint exhaustion. The no-simultaneously-becoming-rid claim is a mere consequence
of Socrates' claim that health and sickness are mutually exclusive in a
subject: since subjects cannot simultaneously *have* both conditions, they
obviously cannot simultaneously *become* rid of both. This weaker claim is
consistent with there being in-between conditions of a subject that are
neither health nor sickness. Thus the apparent contradiction between this
discussion with Callicles and the earlier discussion with Polus is avoided.
Moreover, it is only the weaker claim that Socrates explicitly relies on in
his refutation of Callicles (497d).

Despite these apparent advantages of the weaker interpretation of Socrates' claim, the text rules it out. For in giving an example of his claim in the case of eye disease, he asks, "But what of when a person is rid of eye disease? Is he therefore at that time also rid of eye health, that is (*kai*), at the same time *has he finally become rid* [*teleutôn . . . apêllaktai*] of both?" (496a3–6, emphasis mine). Here the use of the perfect tense rules out the weaker interpretation of Socrates' claim. Moreover, immediately after this passage, as quoted above, Socrates describes the relation as that of being held and released "in turn" (*en merei*) by a subject. The sense is unequivocal: there are two conditions, and the subject is either in one or the other, not both. I conclude that Socrates must be interpreted as claiming joint exhaustion, even on pain of contradiction.

But in fact there is no contradiction. The things that are neither good nor bad are "things in the world" (*ti tôn ontôn*, 467e1–2), "which sometimes share in the good, sometimes the bad, and sometimes neither" (467e7–468a1). Socrates limits his examples of such things to human actions—"sitting, walking, running, and sailing"—and to objects—"stones and timbers" (468a1–3). By contrast, the discussion with Callicles concerns conditions *of a subject*, as the examples all show (health/sickness, ophthalmia/eye health, strength/weakness, swiftness/slowness, 495e–496b). Socrates in the discussion with Polus did not claim that between *every* pair of opposites, including those opposites that are conditions of a subject, there exists an intermediate state that is neither good nor bad. So I can admit on behalf of Socrates that there are in-between things in the world—such as the action *fasting* and the object *dry food* that sometimes contribute to ("share in") health, sometimes to sickness, and sometimes to neither; and meanwhile I may consistently hold that a subject must be either in health or sickness.[4]

Of course, it would be uncharitable to take Socrates to be foolishly insisting that one must either be in perfect health or be a paradigm of some disease or other. But there is no need to interpret in that way his claim that health and sickness are jointly exhaustive in a subject. It is possible to attribute to Socrates the view that health is a standard, determined perhaps by the context of a given conversation; and that I am truly said to be sick insofar as I fail to attain that standard. I take it therefore as established that the relation which Socrates has picked out is that of being mutually exclusive and jointly exhaustive in a subject. This relation does in fact distinguish the desirable from the satisfying, as Socrates claims. Just how it distinguishes the two has not been well understood.

The argument may seem to have a straightforward formulation:

a. The good and the bad are (opposites and hence are) mutually exclusive and jointly exhaustive in a subject.

Socrates establishes the truth of this premise by considering the pairs: doing well/doing poorly, health/sickness, strength/weakness, swiftness/slowness, and happiness/misery (495e–496b).

b. Pleasure and pain are *not* mutually exclusive and jointly exhaustive in a subject.

Socrates establishes the truth of this premise by considering the pair: drinking when thirsty/thirst (496c–e).

c. Therefore, pleasure is not the good (497a).[5]

But this formulation is invalid. To see this, consider that, like pleasure and pain, the good and the desire for good are *not* mutually exclusive and jointly exhaustive in a subject, yet from this fact and premise *a* it does not follow that the good is not the good.

It is true that if I add a tacit premise to *a* and *b* I can validly infer *c*. In particular, conclusion *c* will follow if I add the further premise:

d. If goodness is pleasure, badness is pain.[6]

But is it fair to assume that Callicles ought to accept this premise? The examples of pains he accepts are thirst and hunger, which are, respectively, the desire for drink and food. The proper pair to abstract from Callicles' pairs, (drink, thirst) and (food, hunger) is therefore not (good, bad) but (good, desire for good). Thus Callicles ought to accept not premise *d* but the following:

e. If goodness is pleasure, *desire for goodness* is pain.

Can premise *d* be taken in a way acceptable to Callicles? If "badness" means *desire for goodness*, *d* and *e* will come to the same thing. But now premise *a* must be declared false or else the argument equivocates. (As shall be made clear below, those who rely on tacit premises such as *d* equivocate between *opposites* and *requisites*.) Since premise *d* is unfair to Callicles and is never explicitly advanced by Socrates or accepted by Callicles, I conclude that this version of the argument should not be attributed to Socrates.

At least it follows from premises *a* and *b* that the *pair* (good, bad) is not identical to the *pair* (pleasure, pain).[7] But the non-identity of goodness and pleasure does not follow from the non-identity of these pairs. To see this, consider that the pair (good, bad) is also not identical to the pair (good, desire for good). Since Socrates does not mention pairs, and since the formulation in terms of pairs is invalid anyway, I conclude that this version of the argument should not be attributed to him.

The conclusion *c* does follow if, rather than a pair that contains the good and a pair that contains the pleasant, the argument takes the good with its opposite and the pleasant with its opposite:[8]

f. The good (that is, the intrinsically desirable) and its opposite are mutually exclusive and jointly exhaustive in a subject.

g. Pleasure (that is, the satisfying of appetite) and its opposite are not mutually exclusive and jointly exhaustive in a subject.

c. Therefore, pleasure is not the good.

But there is an objection to this version of the argument, too: it equivocates on "opposite." Regarding premise *f*, I may grant that such things as health and sickness are mutually exclusive and jointly exhaustive in a subject in the same respect at the same time, and I may agree with Socrates (495e6, 469b6) that such things are opposites. Moreover, regarding premise *g*, I may grant that the satisfaction of drinking when thirsty requires the presence of thirst (thus this satisfaction and its appetite are not mutually exclusive); also that it is possible, when I finish drinking, to be neither satisfying myself nor thirsting (thus this satisfaction and its appetite are not jointly exhaustive).

But thirst is not the opposite of the satisfaction of drinking when thirsty (nor, by the way, does Socrates claim it is). If the satisfaction of drinking when thirsty does have an opposite in the sense of premise *f*, it will be the *dis*satisfaction of *not* drinking when thirsty. By way of contrast, I may call thirst the "requisite" of that satisfaction; and if doing well, health, strength, swiftness, or happiness do have requisites in the sense of premise *g*, they will be (not doing poorly but) the desire to do well, (not sickness but) the desire for health, and so on. Thus my objection is that this version of Socrates' argument equivocates on "opposite"; premise *g* must be rejected. Since Socrates does not call pain the opposite of pleasure, and since the formulation in terms of opposites equivocates, I conclude that this version of the argument should not be attributed to him.

Despite the above subtleties, the principle of Socrates' argument is clear. He has picked out a relation by which, he claims, the good is distinguished from the pleasant, according to Callicles' theory. In offering my own interpretation of Socrates' argument, I shall not claim that the dialectic of this passage should be understood as a statement of a proof, nor, it follows, as a statement of an invalid proof that happens to be psychologically persuasive or effective ad hominem (that is, as sophistry). Rather, I read this passage as a discussion to produce understanding in Callicles and the reader of what Socrates' relation is and that the relation does distinguish Callicles' pleasant from the good. To produce understanding is not sophistry nor necessarily logically sound argument; it is pedagogy. Of course, Socrates often produces understanding by giving what logicians call a sound argument. I think Socrates only intends to produce understanding, never to give sound arguments, but the two goals are close enough in practice that it does not usually cause problems to treat Socrates as doing the latter.

The two-place relation that Socrates has picked out is *"being mutually exclusive and jointly exhaustive in a subject with."* As shown, this relation does prove the non-identity of the pair (good, bad) and the pair (pleasure, pain), but does not prove the non-identity of goodness and pleasure. However, if I turn the two-place relation into the one-place predicate *"being mutually exclusive and jointly exhaustive in a subject with the opposite,"* then it does succeed in proving the non-identity of goodness and pleasure. For goodness is mutually exclusive and jointly exhaustive in a subject with its opposite, badness, but pleasure is not so related to pain.

I have already given an objection: Socrates' conclusion that goodness is not the same as pleasure does not follow, unless he claims that such things as drinking when thirsty and thirst are opposites. But they are not, for I have distinguished the *opposite* (the dissatisfaction of not drinking when thirsty) from the *requisite* (thirst). Socrates does not explicitly notice this distinction between opposite and requisite (although he does refrain from calling pain the opposite of pleasure or thirst the opposite of the satisfaction of drinking). But the distinction does not make a difference; the conclusion will still follow.[9]

Let us take the word *opposite* in its precise sense. It remains true that the intrinsically desirable and its opposite are jointly exhaustive (as well as mutually exclusive) in a subject: for example, one must be either healthy or sick. But the satisfying of an appetite and its *opposite* are not jointly exhaustive: for example, it is not the case that one must be either drinking when thirsty or not drinking when thirsty. For someone might escape from thirst altogether: besides the states of drinking when thirsty and of not drinking when thirsty, one might be in the state either of drinking when *not* thirsty or of *not* drinking when not thirsty. So in the strict sense of "opposite," there still is a distinction between the intrinsically desirable and the satisfaction of appetite.

Consider, next, the relation, precisely, of being requisite. It is likely that Socrates was drawing attention to this very relation when he pointed out that "each one of us must cease at the same time from thirsting and from the pleasure of drinking" (trans. Woodhead, 497b; see also 497c–d). For presumably he had not forgotten that one can finish drinking yet continue to thirst. He should be understood there, rather, as claiming that the satisfaction of drinking cannot exist without thirst.

It is possible to misunderstand this claim. There are certainly cases where I can get satisfaction in drinking, yet not be thirsting. For example, there is the satisfaction of participating in a toast, even after thirst has ceased. There is also the pleasure of drinking after thirst has ceased for the sake of the taste of the drink. Again, there is the sybaritic pleasure of drinking *beyond* thirst: when thirst has been satisfied, there is still the pleasure of feeling one's appetitive cup overflow, as it were. But in all such cases the satisfaction is not of thirst but of something else: in my examples, the wish to participate in toasting, the taste (not thirst) for drink, and the wish for a feeling of overflow. So there is a distinction between cases where the satisfaction *is had in* drinking, where thirst is not the requisite, and the cases where the satisfaction *is that of* drinking, and thirst indeed is the requisite.

Once this distinction is understood, the Calliclean must grant that every appetite is requisite to its satisfaction. In Socrates' words, the satisfying must cease when the appetite ceases. The apparent exceptions—drinking to toast, drinking for taste, and "overdrinking"—are seen to prove the rule, for they are satisfactions not of thirst but of, respectively, the appetites to toast, taste, and overflow.

A person, then, cannot be in the state of satisfying an appetite unless that appetite exists. But, it must be conceded, a person *can* be doing well, say financially, without desiring to do so (such a person might in fact actively desire to be doing poorly financially—imagine a case where a greedy tyrant systematically kills or exiles the rich to gain their possessions); a person *can* be in a state of health without having the desire for health (again, such a person might actively desire poor health, for example, when trying to avoid military service by getting a medical exception). There is in almost every case a possibility that the desire for some good state be overridden (all such states are therefore only extrinsically desirable).[10]

There is one qualification to the claim that the desire for any good state can be overridden that Socrates must admit: the case of doing well, not as a moneymaking being or a physiological being, but as a human being. For, according to Socrates, all desire this (*Meno* 78a, *Euthyd.* 278e). But this qualification does not affect the truth that desires are not requisite. Socrates can concede that it never happens that we do well without the desire to do so. The reason it never happens is simply because we never cease to desire to do well, not because a desire is requisite to doing well. *If* there were someone who did not desire to do well as a human being, it *would* be possible for that person to be doing well yet not be desiring to do so.[11]

It follows that, with the strict relation of being requisite, there again is a distinction between the intrinsically desirable and the satisfaction of appetite. For, in the case of satisfaction, it is true that "each one of us must cease at the same time from [the appetite] and from the [satisfaction]" (497c). But, in the case of the desirable, this is false: even in the case of the intrinsically desirable, unconditional desires are not requisite (though in fact ever present). I conclude that Socrates has refuted Callicles' identification of appetite satisfaction with the intrinsically desirable in this passage. For he has succeeded in finding a relation that distinguishes the two.

5.2 The Argument from Pleased Cowards

Socrates' second argument refutes Callicles' identity thesis by showing that it leads to an account of the good man to which there are clear counter-examples. This argument is best understood by comparison with two earlier counter-examples used by Socrates.[12] Callicles had claimed that

a. A man is truly good (as opposed to conventionally good) insofar as he continually satisfies large and intense appetites,

and that

b. A man leads a good life by creating and satisfying large and intense appetites (491e6–492a3).

Socrates replied with two counter-examples: the "scabbing and itching" man who is able to "scratch freely" (494c6–7), and the *kinaidos*, the receptive partner in a homosexual act, who "freely has what he wants" (494e6). "The life spent in scratching" (494c7–8) and "the life of the *kinaidos*" (494e4) are cases where intense appetites are continually created and satisfied but are not thereby cases of good men living well.

The counter-examples, then, establish that

1*a*. There is a man who is not good insofar as he continually satisfies large and intense appetites,

and that

1*b*. There is a man who does not live a good life by creating and satisfying large and intense appetites.

Thus these counter-examples refute Callicles' account of the good man and of the good life. But they do not refute his thesis of the identity of the good (that is, the intrinsically desirable) and the pleasant (that is, the satisfying of the appetite). To see this, assume, as Callicles and Socrates both have, that to be good and live well is intrinsically desirable. It then follows from premise 1*a* that

2*a*. There is a man who does not have something that is intrinsically desirable insofar as he continually satisfies large and intense appetites,

and from premise 1*b* that

2*b*. There is a man who does not have something that is intrinsically desirable by creating and satisfying large and intense appetites.

But neither consequence 2*a* nor consequence 2*b* refute Callicles' identity thesis. For a person may satisfy appetites throughout his life without satisfying all appetites, in particular without satisfying the appetite (if it is an appetite) to live well or to be good.

The argument from pleased cowards, like the counter-examples, will establish the truth of premise 1*a*. Socrates establishes it with the example of the pleased coward, which is an effective example against Callicles. Callicles was able, at least verbally, to make his position accept the lives of the scratcher and *kinaidos* as good. But he is too strongly committed to the virtue of courage to be able, even verbally, to accept cowards as virtuous.[13]

But this argument goes beyond the earlier counter-examples by adding to premise 1*a* the premise that

3. A man is good insofar as good things are present to him (497e1–3, 498d2–3).

Is there any reason for Callicles to accept premise 3?[14] Callicles has claimed that a man is good ("fine and just according to nature") insofar as he continually satisfies large and intense appetites (491e6–492a3). And presumably Callicles takes the statement "good things are present to a man" to be true insofar as a man is satisfying his appetites. Thus understood, he cannot object to premise 3.

By the way, Socrates himself takes "good things are present to a man" to be true insofar as a man possesses what is intrinsically desirable, which, he argues, is nothing but knowledge (*Euthyd.* 278e–281e). And Socrates believes that a man is good insofar as he has knowledge (see for example *La.* 194d1–3). Thus Socrates himself accepts premise 3. (Those who follow Kant in distinguishing between the "moral" use of the word *good* in the expression "good man" and the "technical" use of "good" in "good things" will object to this premise, but that is beside the point: Socrates and Callicles both would deny the distinction.)

Finally, Socrates and Callicles are taking the terms *pleasures* and *the pleasant* as well as *the satisfying of appetites* and *the satisfying of appetite* to be all interchangeable, and that they take *goods* or *good things* and *the good* as well as *intrinsic desirables* and *the intrinsically desirable* to be all interchangeable.

In this way Callicles' identity thesis is again refuted. For from this thesis, their license to interchange terms, and premise 3 it follows that

4. A man is good insofar as he continually satisfies large and intense appetites,

which contradicts premise 1*a*.

5.3 The Result of the Arguments with Callicles

Callicles is a hedonist. He also is a Protagorean about the nature of goodness and desirability (see chapters 3 and 4). One lesson sometimes drawn from Socrates' two arguments is that Callicles is refuted because he is both. Following Aristotle (*NE* I.8 1099a7–15; see also X.5), I might say that the simple truth that refutes him is that the vicious feel pleasure in vicious acts.[15] Given this truth, if I assume (with Polus and Callicles) that the vicious cannot be mistaken about what really gives them pleasure, then I must conclude that hedonism is refuted. Almost all commentators seem to have made this assumption and reached this conclusion. On the other hand, if I assume that there is no ultimate explanation of human values other than in hedonistic terms, then I must conclude that the vicious are mistaken about what really gives them pleasure. Socrates is a hedonist— the evidence lies not only in the *Protagoras* but in the *Gorgias* itself.[16] For Socrates, therefore, the arguments refute not hedonism but Protagoreanism about goodness and desire.

5.4 Summary

Three one-sentence answers have been presented to the question how to live:

S. The best life is spent in getting what one desires.
P. The best life is spent in getting what seems best.
C. The best life is spent in satisfying appetites.

Statement S is affirmed by all three, Socrates, Polus, and Callicles. But Polus believed that talk about desire amounted to nothing but talk about what seems best: he attempted to interpret statement S as equivalent to statement P. Callicles believes that talk about desire amounted to nothing but talk about felt appetites: he attempted to interpret statement S as equivalent to statement C. Both attempts to reinterpret S are versions of Protagoreanism, for both rely on the original or modified claims 1 and 2 that were discussed in section 3.5. Socrates in the *Gorgias* does not argue against statement S but only against statements P and C; indeed he argues against P and C by distinguishing them from S. And statement S is consistent with the scientific hedonism of the *Protagoras*.

Death Is One of Two Things

In preceding chapters I have developed, then refuted, a Calliclean account of pleasure and shown how Socrates can consistently be a hedonist in both the *Protagoras* and the *Gorgias*. But my distinction between two species of hedonism, only one of which Socrates defends, still leaves a problem. In the *Protagoras*, Socrates defends the claim that pleasure is the only good. But in the *Apology* and elsewhere Socrates unquestionably believes that virtue is a good above all others. Socrates cannot, it seems, have it both ways. Either virtue, as in the *Apology*, or pleasure, as in the *Protagoras*, may be the supreme good—but not both. Since the supremacy of virtue is unquestionable for Socrates, it would seem that hedonism is an impossible doctrine for Socrates to hold.

This chapter begins to solve this problem by giving further interpretation of a Socratic account of pleasure. I am already in a position to postulate that Socrates' hedonism is a satisfaction theory of true not felt desire (see section 4.3). Evidence in the *Apology* will show that for Socrates the intrinsically satisfying pleasures of true desire include what I shall call modal pleasures.

One of the most familiar scenes in the history of philosophy is the inspiring picture at the end of Plato's *Apology* of a noble Socrates, his confidence undaunted by the death sentence he has received in trial from fellow citizens. The basis of Socrates' nobility—his remaining at the post where God has assigned him, which was the duty of leading the philosophical life (*Ap.* 28e)—is not generally questioned. But the basis of his confidence has been harder to understand.

Socrates bases his confidence on two grounds. One is a "great sign": Socrates' *daimonion* "could not have failed to oppose" him unless what he was about to do—die—was "something good" (40c). I shall not discuss this basis (see Brickhouse and Smith 1989a: 237–257; Reeve 1989: 180–182).

The other basis is an argument in the form of a constructive dilemma, based on the premise that death is one of two things. This dilemma has been standard fare in introductory philosophy classes and occasionally addressed in professional literature, but its force has been underappreciated. Because of a few stock objections, it is rarely thought convincing or even intellectually respectable: it appears that, if Socrates is giving an argument, "he unintentionally committed errors that college sophomores can readily identify" (Roochnik 1985: 216).

Because the stock objections have appeared obvious and overwhelming, sympathetic interpreters have been driven to reinterpret what is plainly an argument (more precisely, pedagogy; see section 5.1) as "not to be taken literally" (Armleder 1966: 46) or as a complicated piece of dialectic designed to "arouse us to thought," "in contrast to its superficial appearance" (Roochnik 1985: 213). Reeve (1989) leaves a stock objection unanswered, and takes it to show that the argument gives us "only" hope, despite the fact that Socrates says it gives us "much" hope (*Ap.* 40c4). Brickhouse and Smith (1989a: 259, n. 61; likewise 1989b: 156–157) say the argument is intended to "reassure" rather than to "convince," without explaining how one may have any degree of reassurance without a corresponding degree of conviction.[1]

Perhaps all commentators would agree that the argument is meant to persuade at least some who hear or read it. But some commentators suppose that it is hardly meant to persuade real philosophers or thoughtful people. And some might suppose that Socrates is not really arguing that death is a good thing but only that virtue should not be renounced in the face of death.[2] My thesis, by contrast, is that Socrates' argument ought to be taken at face value: he really is arguing that death is a good thing. I defend this thesis by showing that his argument is seriously defensible: there are rational replies to the stock objections. A consequence of my defense is of particular interest to the thesis of this book: I shall be able to draw a useful conclusion about Socrates' account of pleasure.

6.1 The Original Argument

The dilemma form of Socrates' argument is easy to understand in outline. Death is "one of two things," either "nothingness" or a "change and migration of the soul from here to another place" (40c5–9).

In the one case, if death is nothingness, then it is utterly without perception, which is like a dreamless sleep. But there are few days and nights, even for the rich and powerful, which would be "better and pleasanter" than a night of dreamless sleep (40d6). Moreover "all time will appear to be nothing more than a single night" (40e3–4). Thus such a death is a "wonderful gain" (40d1–2).

In the other case, if death is a migration of the soul to another place, "and the stories are true that all the dead are there," then death is an unsurpassed good (40e5–7), an "inconceivable happiness" (41c3–4). For whoever goes there will escape the "so-called judges of this world" and find the "true judges," and will meet sages and heroes, and—"the greatest thing"—Socrates can continue to cross-examine people to see who are really wise and who merely think themselves so.

The conclusion, in either case, is that death is "something good" (40c4–5).

6.2 The False Dilemma Objection

The most common objection is to the premise that death is one of two things, for it seems that death might be any number of things; hence Socrates is unjustified in restricting the options to two. This objection is easily answered or at least shifted elsewhere, since a part of the intuitive problem behind the objection is not fully addressed until the hell objection is considered below.

One thing we know about death is that the body is eventually destroyed. If the soul is not destroyed along with the body (which is the first of Socrates' alternatives), then it has to go somewhere (which is the second). Actually, Socrates claims that it goes somewhere *else*, and it might be thought that this is more than we know: why cannot the soul stay around *here* as a spectral observer? But even spectral observers are, in a sense, cut off from their community, and one of the verbs Socrates uses to describe the change (*apodêmêsai*, 40e4) suggests that *being away from one's community* is a feasible way to understand what he means in the disjunctive premise by "going somewhere else." Immediate reincarnation back into one's community might still be thought to be possible, but such an event would appear to be indistinguishable from nothingness, since, if there is reincarnation, it is evidently with a complete break of psychological and physical continuity. There is a natural way to understand Socrates' disjunction, then, according to which it is truly exhaustive.

6.3 The Deprivation Objection

Socrates needs the conditional premise that if death is nothingness, it is a gain. It is commonly objected that nothingness is deprivation, not pleasure, and hence bad, not good, in the case of all but the most wretched lives. In view of this objection, I will examine the steps Socrates takes from nothingness to gain.

He begins with an unproblematic phenomenological equation of nothingness and a night of dreamless sleep: both events are alike in being utterly without perception. Next Socrates asserts that few human days or nights are more pleasant than a night of undisturbed sleep. It is this assertion that the stock objection has denied. Roochnik (1985: 214), for instance, argues that "the only reason that a night's dreamless sleep is pleasant is because one wakes from it in the morning refreshed and vitalized. Only then can one look back gratefully to the night." The objection is that we find great pleasure only in *waking* from dreamless sleep. Socrates is in effect accused of confusing the pleasure of waking refreshed with the actual senselessness of the sleep, which of course contains no perceptions, and hence no perceptions of pleasure.

But this objection, not Socrates' argument, is what is confused. Following Hume, the British utilitarians, and Moore, this objection conceives all pleasure as sensation and ignores the ancient Greek distinction drawn by Aristotle (*NE* VII.11–14). That distinction is between what I shall call *modal* and *sensate* pleasures. Modal pleasures are things that are done or happen *in a certain way*: (1) they are done or happen effortlessly or without boredom, or (2) are approached in a certain way, or (3) have a particular value to a person. By contrast, sensate pleasures are the feelings that result from what is done or happens.[3]

Ryle (1949: 108) is one of those responsible for reintroducing philosophy to this distinction. Ryle reminds us that the enjoyment of pleasure is not limited to the feeling of sensation:

> Doubtless the absorbed golfer experiences numerous flutters and glows of
> rapture, excitement and self-approbation in the course of his game. But
> when asked whether or not he had enjoyed the periods of the game be-

tween the occurrences of such feelings, he would obviously reply that he had, for he had enjoyed the whole game.

The "whole game" is a modal pleasure; the "numerous flutters and glows" are sensate pleasures. As another example shows, neither a particular event nor a particular feeling are necessarily pleasures:

> Even though what a person has felt is properly described as a thrill of plea-sure or, more specifically, as a tickle of amusement, it is still a proper ques-tion whether he not only enjoyed the joke but also enjoyed the tickled feel-ing that it gave him. Nor should we be much surprised to hear him reply that he was so much delighted by the joke that the "tickled" feeling was quite uncomfortable. (Ryle 1949: 109)

My hypothesis is that Socrates' argument makes no assertion about the sensate pleasure that is derived during or as a result of undisturbed sleep. His assertion is that a night's dreamless sleep is a hard-to-surpass modal pleasure.

Given that there is a distinction between modal and sensate pleasure, and that Socrates is making an assertion about modal pleasure, I can now examine the plausibility of Socrates' claim. I listed above three well-accepted criteria for modal pleasure, and a night's dreamless sleep is a plea-sure according to all three. (1) The first criterion—happening effortlessly and without boredom—is probably the most important of the three, and it is here that a night's undisturbed sleep has the greatest success. For indeed it is the circumstance that is most effortless and least susceptible to boredom, as Socrates shows by looking at things from the point of view of eternity. "All time will appear to be nothing more than a single night" (*Ap.* 40e3–4). Suppose we have the power of extending any particular modal pleasure indefinitely. If a pleasure we can effortlessly enjoy only for a little while is inferior to one we can enjoy for a long time, then clearly sleep is at the top of the list. Moreover, (2) a night's sound sleep can be approached with great anticipation. There is evidence that Socrates ap-proached death with the greatest anticipation. Much of the *Phaedo*, very likely, is an exposition of middle Plato's metaphysics rather than a report of Socrates' last day. But, even though the metaphysics there is inaccu-rately attributed to Socrates, I am less inclined to take as inaccurate that dialogue's report that Socrates felt unsurpassed anticipation on that day (*Pho.* 84c–85b). Finally, (3) sleep is valued for its ability to release us from worry and pain. There are grounds to attribute to Socrates a recognition of this value. In the *Gorgias* he argues that bodily pleasures by their very nature require, intermingled, bodily pains. For example, requisite to the pleasure of quenching is the pain of parching (*Grg.* 496e, see also *Pho.* 60b–c). According to these criteria, then, the nothingness of death, like sleep, will be not a mere modal pleasure but, according to the first criterion, unsurpassed and, according to the second and third criteria, hard to surpass in proportion to how strongly Socrates anticipates death and to how valuable he finds a release from bodily care and pain. Notice, nonetheless, that Socrates is not arguing that death is the only good or pleasure, nor that it is unsurpassable, but only that it is better than most of the sorts of pleasures and goods human beings are capable of experiencing.

Despite the success with which a night of dreamless sleep meets these three criteria of modal pleasure, there might be other conditions which show that sleep fails to be a pleasure. Thanks to Ryle's golfing example, we have seen that it is false that in order for some circumstance *C* to be a pleasure, one must consciously feel sensations of pleasure in *C's* happening. But in order for *C* to be a pleasure, must not one at least (1) be conscious that *C* is happening, or at the very least (2) be conscious? I suspect that people who are tempted by conditions 1 or 2 are still under the sway of the crude idea that pleasure must be sensate. For both conditions are in conflict with what appears to be the case: there are the widespread, daily reports people make that they have enjoyed a good night's sleep or an afternoon's nap. The confused theorist might think that these reports refer to the feeling of refreshment these people had upon waking and likewise ought to think that the golfer's report of enjoying the game refers only to the flutters and glows actually sensed during the game. But the rest of us will recognize the possibility of a golfer enjoying the game while feeling nothing but aches and pains, and the possibility of enjoying a sound sleep but waking with a headache or in a depression. So I find these conditions hardly compelling.

Moreover, there are counter-examples to the first of these conditions even apart from the pleasures of sleep. Consider the experience of being totally absorbed in an activity. Sometimes lovers of fiction can almost lose themselves in the plot of a good book; they are barely aware that they are reading. Other times they do lose themselves in the plot and are unaware they are reading. Condition 1 would have us say, absurdly, that only the first readers are enjoying the story. Such absorption, of course, can take place in almost any activity or circumstance; all such cases are counter-examples to condition 1.

Other examples will make condition 2 look implausible. There are a variety of states in which the subject, though not fully or perhaps not at all conscious, may enjoy modal pleasures of the most extreme nature. Dodds (1951) describes the following, all of which would have been known to Socrates, some of which he participated in: prophetic mania (p. 69), ecstatic bacchanals (p. 76), infectious orgiastic dance (pp. 78–79, 272: attributed to Socrates by Dodds on the basis of *Euthyd.* 277d), inspired poetic frenzy (pp. 80–82), the madness of Eros (p. 218), and dissociated states of mental withdrawal (p. 222: attributed to Socrates at *Symp.* 174d–175c, 220c–d). I see no reason to suppose that consciousness is essential to these activities (except perhaps mental withdrawal) in order for them to be modal pleasures; thus it appears unjustifiable to insist on consciousness as a condition of pleasure. Finally, it is noteworthy that the *Philebus*, though a later dialogue, assumes that one can coherently talk of a person unconsciously enjoying pleasure (*Phlb.* 21a–b).

Consider next a genuinely necessary condition of modal pleasure: in order for some circumstance C to be a pleasure, there must be a subject of C (even if that subject need not be conscious of C or conscious at all). This condition, unlike conditions 1 and 2, allows us, as it should, to call undisturbed sleep a pleasure, for one exists as the subject of one's sleep, even though unconscious. But it appears to rule out death as a pleasure, for by hypothesis death is nothingness; hence there seems to be no subject to enjoy death. There are two replies Socrates might make to this objection, one practical and one metaphysical.

The practical reply is to point out that death (whether or not it has a subject) and an eternal dreamless sleep (which of course has a subject) will be, for all practical purposes, indistinguishable. Of course if Socrates, having supposed death is nothingness, went on to assert death was an eternal sleep, he would be contradicting himself. But he makes no such assertion; he merely says death is "like" sleep (*Ap.* 40d1). Since death will be practically indistinguishable from a great pleasure, he can plausibly regard death as a good thing.

The metaphysical reply is that a given person's death, say Socrates', does have a subject, namely, Socrates. Though the point is controversial, I myself readily concede to the metaphysical tradition founded by Parmenides, explored by Plato, and extending through Quine, that there are insuperable problems in referring to a subject that does not in any way exist. (Socrates' own reaction to this point, when used to support a paradox of false speech, is portrayed at *Euthyd.* 284b–287d.) But past existence is a metaphysically allowable subject (see, for example, Yourgrau 1987). Just as millennia of other historical effects can be legitimately attributed to Socrates, who exists only in the past, so too can the ongoing condition of his being dead be attributed to him as subject.

There is a final necessary condition of modal pleasure that might raise a problem. The case could be made that I, following Ryle, have given above only incidental criteria of modal pleasure—happening without effort or boredom, approached with anticipation and having some value to one's life—mere symptoms, as it were. The real nature of modal pleasure is seen by Aristotle and is what explains why it has these characteristics: modal pleasure is "unimpeded activity of the soul" (*NE* VII.11–14). Such activity of the soul, namely, the exercise of a capacity central to doing well as a human being, explains the absorbing, eagerly anticipated value of modal pleasure (this explanation is suggested by Dent 1984: 42–43). But being dead, however effortless it might be, does not appear to exercise any such capacity of the human being. Hence being dead is not a modal pleasure.

To this objection the practical reply can again be made. For all practical purposes, death and modal pleasure will be indistinguishable. Of course, if Socrates, having supposed death is nothingness, went on to assert death was (rather than was like) a modal pleasure, he would be contradicting himself. But he makes no such assertion.

But I am more tempted by a pious reply. On the hypothesis that death is nothingness, it follows that human beings are mortals. Hence to be dead is central to our nature; indeed it is life that is the wonderful anomaly, as Pindar saw in characterizing us as "ephemerals" and "dream of shadow" (*Pyth.* viii). Being dead, then, will after all turn out to be the condition most appropriate to our nature. To insist on more would be the height of impiety, mortal pretense to immortality. I see no problem in attributing such an understanding of our place as mortals to Socrates (see *Ap.* 23a5–7). And on such an understanding Socrates is justified, I think, in saying death is or is like a great pleasure.

6.4 An Ad Hominem Objection

A stock ad hominem objection is that Socrates claims at 29b (see also 42a) that he is like all men in that he does not sufficiently know about the things in Hades; however, unlike other men he does not believe he does know them. He knows that he does not know. It appears inconsistent for such a person to advance an argument that death is a good thing. The reply, as other commentators have seen, is that the inconsistency disappears if we distinguish "knowledge" from "reasons for hope" (Ehnmark 1946: 115), or "having a definite view" from "having certain knowledge" (Hoerber 1966: 92).[4]

6.5 The Hell Objection

Socrates' second conditional premise seems to be that if death is a migration, it is a chance to cross-examine the heroes, hence an unsurpassed good.

The stock objection is to point out that there is no reason to suppose the soul's migration will be to any such desirable place. Socrates ought to consider the possibilities, recognized in Greek literature, of varieties of hell for an afterlife. Roochnik (1985: 214) paraphrases the dead Achilles to beautiful purpose: "perhaps the dead Socrates will discover that he would rather be a simpleton on noisy earth than a philosopher king in dim Hades." I shall develop three replies to this objection—logical, ethical, and theological.

The Logical Reply

There is a strictly logical reply that will appeal to many with a demythologizing cast of mind. These will insist that of course death is nothingness. Given that death *is* nothingness, it follows by logic that, if it is *not* nothingness, it is the particular sort of migration Socrates describes.

There are a couple of reasons not to ascribe this justification to Socrates, even if it justifies his argument. First, it is anachronistic to suppose that Socrates would put stock in the unintuitive logical inference required by this reply. And second, in the *Phaedrus* (229b–230a) and the *Apology* itself (26c–e), we see him scornful of the demythologizing mind that the logical reply requires.

The Ethical Reply

The ethical reply justifies Socrates' inference that the afterlife will not be harmful as a consequence of his ethical thesis that the good man cannot be harmed, which follows from his argument in *Republic* I that the righteous are happy. I interpret and defend this argument in chapter 8. This reply may save the conclusion that death is good or at least harmless; it hardly justifies the inference that migration of the soul will be a good as great as any Socrates can imagine.

The Theological Reply

The theological reply justifies Socrates' inference by adding the premise that God is good. Suppose there is a migration of the soul after death. This is extraordinary and confirms the stories that are told to the extent that they assign an afterlife to human beings. The problem is that the stories conflict about the desirability and goodness of the afterlife. Why is Socrates willing to believe that if there is an afterlife, it will be an unsurpassed good? How can he give credence to the traditional stories and at the same time revise them so arbitrarily? In the *Euthyphro*, we see Socrates engaged in a confident revision of traditional religious beliefs parallel to the revision of traditional afterlife beliefs in the *Apology*. In the *Apology*, Socrates confidently revises the ambiguous stories so that the afterlife becomes an unsurpassed good; in the *Euthyphro*, Socrates just as confidently revises the stories that the gods can quarrel and fight each other. In neither dialogue does Socrates explain the principle by which he makes his revision.

In *Republic* II Socrates makes the same complaints as in the *Euthyphro*: that he cannot believe the traditional myths, recorded in Hesiod's *Theogony* (secs. III and VIII), of father gods (Uranus and Cronus) hating their divine sons (Cronus and Zeus) and those sons rebelling with violence against their fathers' injustices (*Euthphr.* 6a, *Rep.* II 377e–378a), nor that, in general, gods war with gods (*Euthphr.* 6b–c, *Rep.* II 378b–c). In complaining in the *Republic*, Socrates again fails to give a reason for his confidence in calling traditional stories lies, but immediately after the complaint, when he begins to say what the right pattern of speech about God is, he at last gives a reason: God is good (379b). From the goodness of God he immediately infers that God is always to be spoken of as such, that God does not cause harm or evil (and hence does not cause all things), but does cause welfare and all good things (379b-c).

Although *Republic* II is not classified as a portrayal of the Socrates of the early dialogues (but notice that Vlastos 1991: 162–163 appears so to use it), I postulate that nonetheless Socrates would justify his revisions of traditional stories in both the *Euthyphro* and the *Apology* on the same principle of divine goodness. There is certainly no conflict in supposing that on this point the early and middle Socrates would agree. Though we never see the early Socrates construct an argument from the goodness of God, in at least seven passages he argues from the goodness of virtue.[5] Moreover, such a principle would justify the unargued assertion he makes immediately after the "death is one of two things" argument, that "nothing can harm a good man either in life or after death, and his fortunes are not a matter of indifference to the gods" (*Ap.* 41d1–2).[6]

I will therefore take Socrates to be implicitly relying on the premise of divine goodness. He says (in 40e4–7): "If death is a migration from here to some other place, and the stories are true that all the dead are there, what greater good than this can there be?" I can give the following reconstruction of his argument.[7]

1. Death is a migration to another place (by hypothesis).
2. Therefore the traditional stories are true to say that the dead are in that other place.

Premise 2 can be read in an innocuous sense: let the other place consist of wherever the dead go. Such a reading postpones the Sisyphus/Tantalus objection: why does Socrates think the dead will be able to have conversation with each other in that other place?[8] As things stand, following premise 2 there is a gap that must be filled in before reaching the conclusion:

n. Thus death is a good as great as any Socrates can imagine.

Death, on the migration hypothesis, is not merely something good but a good as great as any Socrates can imagine. This is shown by Socrates' rhetorical question, "What greater good than this can there be?" quoted above.

The text of 40e4–7 is as plain as one could like in committing Socrates to this incomplete argument: I cannot agree with attempts to demote this argument to speculation or rhetoric. But the next section of text, 40e7–41c4, just as plainly, is merely speculating on possible particular forms the afterlife might take: I agree here with Brickhouse and Smith (1989b: 157) that in this passage "Socrates does not pretend to be offering his jurors an exhaustive analysis of the possibilities." Indeed, Socrates does not explicitly claim that he will find the true judges presiding there, nor that he will meet Orpheus, Musaeus, Hesiod, and Homer there, nor that he will meet heroes who died through unjust trials, nor even that he will continue cross-examining there. Socrates' rhetorical questions in this passage allow me to attribute to him only conditional claims:

C1. If one finds the true judges presiding in court there, it will not be unrewarding to die (40e7–41a5).

C2. If one meets Orpheus, Musaeus, Hesiod, and Homer there, it will be worth dying many times (41a6–8).

C3. If Socrates meets heroes who met their death through unfair trials and can compare his fortunes with theirs, it will be especially interesting and rather pleasant for him (41a8–b5).

C4. If Socrates continues cross-examining there as here, it will be the greatest pleasure; if one questions the heroes, it will be worth giving anything; if one talks, mixes, and argues with them, it will be inconceivable happiness (41b5–c4).

Socrates amplifies the conditional claim C4 with a last inference from the traditional stories: if the stories are true, the dead will never die again; therefore the dead are not put to death again for cross-examining others (41c4–7).

This is all the text has to say. So the interpretive problem now takes this form: can I plausibly attribute additional premises to Socrates that will give him a plausible argument from premises 1 and 2 to conclusion n? As it happens, the following premises, if true, will give him a sound argument.

3. To cross-examine the dead would be a good as great as any Socrates can imagine.
4. Death allows one to cross-examine the dead.

Can I plausibly attribute premises 3 and 4 to Socrates? The conditional claim $C4$ indicates Socrates' great attraction to premise 3. He calls cross-examination "the greatest" (*to megiston*, 41b5) pleasure, which, if done with heroes, is something worth giving anything for (*epi posô(i) d' an tis dexaito*, 41b7–8), an "inconceivable happiness" (*amêchanon eudaimonias*, 41c4–5). These same passages, I take it, demonstrate that Socrates would at least like to believe premise 4.

The next question is whether premises 3 and 4 are in themselves plausible. Against premise 3 one might raise what I shall call the heaven objection. The afterlife might be a good, even the best place without being a forum for cross-examination. God, according to this objection, might not harm Socrates in the least by precluding any opportunity for him to cross-examine.[9] I shall consider two versions of this objection: reincarnation and beatitude. Before going into the details of this objection, it is important to note that, unlike the other objections, the heaven objection does not damage Socrates' argument. Even if I succeed in showing Socrates that something surpasses cross-examination, his conclusion, that death is something good, will still follow.

For suppose I show Socrates that there is an F that surpasses cross-examination. He can merely recast his argument by revising premises 3 and 4:

3′. To F would be a good as great as any Socrates can imagine.
4′. Death allows one to F.

The conclusion n will still follow.

Recall that, although Socrates does explicitly assert premises 1 and 2, he does not mention 3 or 4. I am inclined, therefore, to attribute to him only the weaker premises 3′ and 4′ with the addition, inessential to his argument, that a likely candidate for F is cross-examination. That he does not explicitly formulate an argument using premises 3 and 4 may be due to his modest evaluation of his ability to know what death holds. There may be unknown *F*'s of all kinds, and to argue that the afterlife selected for us by God must be cross-examination would perhaps be the sort of conceit of wisdom Socrates rightly condemns at *Apology* 29b. Therefore, on this interpretation, I can explain how to attribute to Socrates a plausible argument that death is good—from premises 1, 2, 3′, and 4′—also why he leaves what has appeared to be a gap at a critical point of his statement of the argument and merely speculates there, and finally how he can consistently argue that death is good while affirming that it is the worst sort of ignorance to claim to know what death is.

Regarding premise 4′, I will reconsider the hell objection. The theological reply, in the ad hominem context of Socrates' trial, is invincible. Any prosecutor who is charging Socrates with impiety must concede that God is good. It follows, as seen in *Republic* II, that God does not cause harm or evil, but does cause welfare and all good things. Consequently, insofar as philosophical cross-examination or some still greater good *F* promotes the good for human beings, piety requires that Socrates will be allowed to engage in such good activities. Moreover, the ethical reply, defended in chapter 8, assures Socrates that he is safe from harm without making theistic assumptions.

Although the heaven objection to premise 3′ does not damage Socrates' argument that death is something good, it is still edifying to consider it. For if Socrates is right to suppose that philosophical cross-examination is a good as great as any we can imagine, it adds to his defense: if God is beneficent in allowing the dead to engage in cross-examination, surely Socrates cannot be doing wrong to allow the Athenians the same opportunity. With these remarks in mind, then, I will consider two versions of the heaven objection.

Version 1: it is arguable that reincarnation may better improve the soul than cross-examination, if one's character flaws are corrected by fitting them to our next life, as in *Republic* X. Plato, by the time of the *Republic*, had given up the Socratic doctrine of the impossibility of *akrasia*. He had become convinced that there is a non-rational element to the soul and as a result that the process of soul improving requires conditioning the non-rational part as well as educating the rational part. On such a bipartite view of the soul pure cross-examination might come off as second best to the improvements brought upon the non-rational part of the soul by some form of non-rational conditioning such as, in a typical case, being reincarnated for a thousand years as a wild boar. The reply to this version is that Plato is wrong about the soul; Socrates is right that *akrasia* is impossible; hence cross-examination is superior (see section 3.2 of this book).

Version 2: God may be capable of magically improving the soul. It is arguably better to be improved by magic than to work for an eternity at trying to improve ourselves through cross-examination. For the product, that is, the state of being perfectly improved, is better than the process of improving. There are a number of possible replies. An Aristotelian reply is that the self that would enjoy beatitude is hard to identify with me (though perhaps after enough cross-examination I could graduate to beatitude). As Aristotle remarks: "No one chooses to possess the whole world if he has first to become someone else (for that matter, even now God possesses the good)" (*NE* IX.4 1166a 20–21, trans. Ross). Whatever the merits of this reply, it cannot be attributed to Socrates, who would choose for himself and everyone else even a self-destructive transformation to the good (*Euthyd.* 285a–c). The Lessing-Kierkegaard reply (see Kierkegaard, *Postscript* II.ii.4) is to insist that there is a greater value in a soul improving than in a soul made perfect. But this reply seems to me incoherent, and it is certainly not Socratic, as the passage just cited in the *Euthydemus* shows. Yet another reply can be taken from Taylor (1982: 113):

> Plainly the gods don't need human help in creating and maintaining the natural world, assuming those to be divine tasks. But there is one good product which they can't produce without human assistance, namely, good human souls. For a good human soul is a self-directed one, one whose choices are informed by its knowledge of and love of the good.

Although Taylor ascribes this view to Socrates, it strikes me as un-Socratic. *Meno* 99e–100a (which may however be ironic) shows Socrates willing to allow that the gods can directly produce good human souls.

I think the best reply is this. Until one's soul has been perfected, magically or otherwise, there is no greater benefit for it than cross-examination. But after one's soul has been perfected, it will remain true that there is no greater conceivable pleasure nor higher good for a human being than the activity of philosophical cross-examination, especially when done with perfect expertise.

6.6 Conclusion

Socrates gives a defensible argument that death is something good. A charitable reading of his argument shows that he thinks of pleasure as modal. While Socrates does not deny that sensate pleasures are also pleasures, he disregards their value as compared to modal pleasures. In chapter 4, I interpreted Socrates to hold a satisfaction hedonism of true desire: goodness consists in the satisfaction of desires I truly have. I may now, as a result of the present chapter, interpret Socrates further on the nature of my true desires as a human being: they are desires for modal pleasures, which are those unimpeded activities that exercise the capacity central to doing well as a human being. In chapter 8, I shall identify that capacity as virtue or righteousness, producing an account of pleasure and virtue that will reconcile Socrates the hedonist with Socrates the virtue supremacist (chapter 10). But next, in chapter 7, I argue that modal hedonism, as opposed to sensate hedonism, is not only Socrates' account of hedonism but is also a compelling account of hedonism.

SEVEN

The Intrinsic Value of
Sense Pleasure and Pain

I presented evidence in chapters 3 and 4 that pleasure, on Socrates' account, is not Protagorean (or Cartesian), that is, it has a real nature apart from what seems pleasant to each subject, and about which the subject can therefore be in error. In chapter 5 I showed Protagorean (such as Calliclean) pleasure to lack intrinsic prudential value, and in chapter 6 I have argued that modal pleasures are valuable in Socrates' account. I shall turn in chapter 8 to the issue of what sort of activities are intrinsically valuable and how they count as true human pleasures (they will turn out to be the righteous activities). But in the present chapter I interpret and defend Socrates' account of sensate pleasure and pain. Since, after all, sensate pleasure and pain are of paramount action-guiding concern to most people, we may ask Socrates what sort of account he gives of them. What if any intrinsic value can Socrates attribute to them? Epicurean lovers of sensations (represented in this chapter by Irwin Goldstein) will find Socrates' restriction of pleasure's value to modal (in particular, moral) activity incredible. They will ask for Socrates (who is assisted in this chapter by Richard Kraut) to consider their own candidate for intrinsic value, sensations. Upon examination, it will, however, result that whatever value sensations have is not in their being sensations but in their being activities. This result is particularly pleasing to the thesis of this book: Socrates' modal as opposed to sensate hedonism will be not only consistent with his argument about death in the *Apology* (as shown in chapter 6) but also compelling in its own right.

Kraut (1994), in the tradition of Stoicism, finds that sensate pleasures have no intrinsic value. Goldstein (1980 and 1989), in the tradition of Epicureanism, finds that they have.[1] I shall follow the traditional usage, in the following discussion, of letting "pleasure" and "pain," unless explicitly identified as *modal*, refer to *sensate* pleasure and pain. In their approach to this issue, both Kraut and Goldstein explicitly reject accounts that make a thing valuable merely because desired (this is indeed the main thesis of Kraut; see also Goldstein 1980: 352–353); an object can be valuable independently of being desired or valued by human beings. In this way, both are Platonic ("objective" or "realistic") rather than Protagorean ("subjective" or "anthropometric") in their understanding of value.

7.1 Empirical Considerations

A traditional Epicurean argument concludes that pleasure is valuable from the premise that there is a striking correlation between sense pleasure and what all animals, including human beings, seek. Both Epicurus (according to Cicero, *de Fin*. I.xxx) and Mill (*Utilitarianism*, ch. 4 para. 3) make this argument. This form of argument can be traced back to Eudoxus (according to Aristotle, *NE* X.2), who "thought pleasure was the good because he saw all things . . . aiming at it."

Aristotle remarks that Eudoxus's arguments "were credited more because of the excellence of his character than for their own sake." So doubts about this argument have been around about as long as the argument itself. A traditional Stoic reply to the Epicurean's empirical consideration is that animals, infants, and human beings seek far more than pleasure, including bodily integrity, freedom of action, and in the case of human beings, mental activity (Cicero, *de Fin*. II.xi). Such a reply may weaken the Epicurean conclusion that pleasure is the *only* ultimate intrinsic value, but it would not affect the conclusion that pleasure is *one* intrinsic value.

A more effective reply to the Eudoxan argument (suggested by Cicero at *de Fin*. II.xi) is that this sort of empirical consideration cannot establish that pleasure, or indeed whatever is pursued, has intrinsic value. For it may be pursued owing to its consequences or accompaniments—it possesses only extrinsic value—or owing to widespread ignorance of its true nature—it possesses only seeming value. Hence the inference from "desired" to "intrinsically desirable" is weak.

Goldstein (1980: 352–353) likewise evaluates the Eudoxan argument as invalidly inferring "x is desirable" from "x is desired." His rejection of the argument follows G. E. Moore and depends on an ontology of meanings about which philosophers make grammatical or lexicographical remarks: "'Desirable' and 'good' do not mean simply 'desired' but '*worthy* or *deserving* of being desired.'"[2] I take him to agree with the underlying Stoic diagnosis, though he couches it with different metaphysical assumptions. If empirical observation is the witness, consideration of its testimony alone provides insufficient grounds to render a verdict about the intrinsic value of pleasure or pain.

7.2 Phenomenological Considerations

A second Epicurean argument is to claim that sense pleasure is judged good and pain evil by the senses themselves (*sensibus ipsis iudicari voluptatem bonum esse, dolorem malum*, Cicero, *de Fin.* II.xii). Goldstein appears to accept a qualified version of this argument.[3] "Our reason for hating pain lies . . . in the very quality of the experience. *The nature of the experience* is our reason for disliking pain, and that is the end of the matter" (1980: 357). Again, "that in itself *every* pleasure is good and *every* pain, broadly conceived, bad, . . . should appear obvious," so that the only task needed, he thinks, is "to get rid of the obstacles to the admission of the obvious" (1989: 257). In terms of Cicero's courtroom metaphor, the classical Epicurean makes sense experience the very *judge* of value, whereas Goldstein makes sense experience the *witness* whose testimony alone is sufficient for a verdict to be rendered by our rational faculty. For Goldstein, accordingly, while the mere empirical data that animals are attracted to pleasure provide insufficient evidence, nonetheless, the mere phenomenological data are, on his account, sufficient and obviously so.

The traditional Stoic reply to the Epicurean is that the senses can at best tell us that pleasure is pleasant, not that it is good. The senses themselves tell us only such things as "sweetness, sourness, smoothness, roughness." Thus whoever assigns jurisdiction about the goodness of pleasure to the senses assigns improper authority to them (Cicero, *de Fin.* II.xii). By extrapolation, then, I can predict that the Stoic reply to Goldstein would be that whoever determines solely from the testimony of the senses that pleasure is good and pain evil reads more into the testimony than can be found there.

Kraut puts the Stoic point this way. When we distinguish the sensation itself of pain (or pleasure) from attendant injury, interruption, or loss of attention or energy, it is apparent that there are no features intrinsic to the sensation itself that justify its being called bad (or good). It is a fact that humans normally dislike (or like) the sensations, but it in no way follows that the sensations contain bad- (or good-) making features. Kraut supports this claim by considering other non-painful sensations, "for example, foul odors and grating noises," which are likewise normally disliked but, when distinguished from attendant distractions are themselves by inspection apparently seen not to be intrinsically bad.

7.3 Considerations of Explanatory Necessity

Another argument of Goldstein's starts with the familiar Epicurean premise that all animals seek pleasure and avoid pain. As discussed, Goldstein does not directly conclude that pleasure is desirable and good and pain undesirable and bad. Instead he follows Findlay (1961: 177) in requiring an explanation of the otherwise "gross, empirical accident" that we uniformly seek pleasure and avoid pain (Goldstein 1980: 350). The explanation Goldstein gives is that sense pleasure and pain have intrinsic value. But first he argues that explanations other than his own are failures.

The Tautological Explanation

We might try to explain the otherwise "gross, empirical accident" by making it tautologous. "Pleasure" means *whatever is sought*; "pain" *whatever is avoided*. But Goldstein (1980: 351) rightly points out that not any sensation can be a pain:

> There clearly is some limit on the sort of sensation that can be an itch or a pain. As pleasure is connected with a desire to seek the experience, so an itch is connected with a desire to scratch. But not just any sensation could be an itch with the mere addition of a desire to scratch the area. Nor could just any sensation be a pain. Brush your cheek lightly with your finger and you feel a light sensation which is neither pleasant nor unpleasant. That sensation would never be an intense pain, nor even a mild pain, whatever desire [to seek or avoid] you might introduce.

The Evolutionary Explanation

We might try to explain the otherwise "gross, empirical accident" with a causal hypothesis: pain is correlated with harm and thus a dislike of pain has survival advantage. Processes of evolution therefore have over time caused aversion to pain. Goldstein (1980: 359–360) criticizes this sort of account. "Within this explanation of the origin of our dislike, it is a primitive, unexplained fact that pain already happened to be correlated with harm. But how is it that pain came to be correlated with harm in the first place?" Goldstein's question, if unanswered, shows an explanatory gap in accounts that try to avoid attributing intrinsic value to pleasure and pain.

Brute Intrinsic Value as an Explanation

Goldstein (1980: 361) suggests that the proper explanation can be found by admitting the intrinsic value of pleasure and pain.

> Nature, through evolutionary forces, chose pain over pleasant or tingling sensations to be correlated with harm because pain, being bad and worth avoiding on its own account, is something creatures have reason to avoid on its own merit.

Unfortunately, Goldstein's account contains its own explanatory gap. Although it explains why pain is correlated with harm, it fails to explain why pain is evil and pleasure good. For Goldstein these are brute, non-tautologous facts; accordingly, they seem to me, on his account, "gross empirical accidents." So the advantage of his account over the competing evolutionary account is not clear, insofar as both contain explanatory gaps.

There is a better account to be given, I believe. It is an account that will not make the value of pleasure and pain mysterious brute facts, and an account that will answer Goldstein's question how pain came to be correlated with harm in the first place.

7.4 A Representational Account
of Pleasure and Pain

Socrates draws an analogy between vision and pleasure at *Protagoras* 356d–e.[4] In the case of both vision and pleasure there is a bodily faculty with "the capacity to produce subjective experience" (*hê tou phainomenou dunamis*) of magnitude. Because of the effects of proximity (whether in space or time), each receptive faculty (whether it receives visible or pleasurable appearances) can make the larger seem smaller and the smaller seem larger (*Prt.* 356c5–6). I take it that the existence of such a capacity for receiving impressions of pleasure and pain must be admitted in view of the notorious fact that it is possible for pleasures and pains to appear greater or smaller than they are (this point is made by Mooradian 1995: 103).[5]

The analogy can be elaborated by other similarities. As Goldstein (1994: 50) points out, sensations of pleasure and pain, like visible perceptions, have duration and felt location. Hume (bk. I pt. 4 sec. 2 of the *Treatise*) notices the involuntary nature, superior force, and "violence" of pleasure, pain, and perception vis à vis memories and abstract ideas.

Socrates asserts that this faculty of sensation can do the following (*Prt.* 356d4–7):

a. Mislead (*eplana*) the soul in its actions and choices concerned with magnitudes. It is for this reason, as Mooradian (1995: 110–112) points out, that such visions and felt pleasures can be categorized as false in the *Philebus*.

b. Disorient (*epoiei anô te kai katô*) the soul. The faculty of vision can cause the sun, for example, to appear bigger and brighter than many stars in relation to which it is in fact smaller and dimmer. The faculty that senses pleasure can make slumping in a chair seem a greater pleasure than good posture.

c. Cause the soul to be constantly accepting and rejecting (*pollakis metalambanein kai metamelein*) the same things. As Nussbaum (1986: 53) has pointed out, this condition of the soul is well illustrated by the Sentry's first speech in Sophocles' *Antigone*: he vacillated between bearing self-incriminating news to Agamemnon and being derelict in his duty to bring it.

d. Produce appearances (*phantasmata*) that rule our choices and actions. I interpret these appearances to include the raw feel of particular pleasures and pains that, by being present or expected, can cause us, say, to take more than our share of the ice cream bombe (J. L. Austin's example, 1979: 198, n. 1) or pull an arm out of the fire, as Mucius, remarkably, did not (Livy, *Ab Urbe Condita* II.13, referred to by Seneca, *De Providentia* III.5).

e. Make life unsafe. The possibly disastrous consequences of a life guided by the mere capacity to sense pleasures and pains are obvious.

The above examples illustrate the range of objects represented by sensate pleasure and pain: slumping in a chair or sitting with good posture; bearing self-incriminating news to one's king or being derelict in one's duty to bring it; taking more than one's share of something like ice cream or pulling away from something like an arm-burning fire. Socrates draws a contrast between the receptive faculty (*hê tou phainomenou dunamis*, whether the capacity to sense visible objects or to sense pleasures and pains), which produces sometimes misleading appearances of magnitudes, and the soul's skill of measurement (*hê metrêtikê technê*, 356d4) of the magnitudes represented by those appearances.

Socrates draws this same sort of contrast between a bodily receptive faculty and the soul's skill in other places. In the *Crito* he contrasts "the reasoning which seems best to my intellect" (*tô[i] logô[i] hos an moi logizomenô*[*i*] *beltistos phainetai*, 46b5–6) with being frightened at the prospect of imprisonment, execution, or confiscation of property, "the way children are frightened by tales of witches who eat children" (*hôsper paidas hêmas mormoluttêtai*, 46c4–5). In the *Phaedo* (99a1–4) he contrasts his own discernment (*hôimên*) of what is right with the "opinion (*doxês*) of what is best" had by his "sinews and bones." In the *Gorgias* (473d–e) Socrates says that Polus, in describing the horrors of physical torture, death, and outrages to wife and children, is not refuting (*ouk elegcheis*) but merely frightening with nursery tales (*mormoluttê*[*i*] *au*). Earlier in the *Gorgias*, Socrates has elaborated this distinction between, on the one hand, the capacity to make flesh creep or mouth water, a capacity that fails to be a skill, and on the other hand, the skill that ministers to what is best, cognizant of the nature of its object and that object's good (464b–465a). Those who lack the rational powers of soul—children or grown-ups as senseless as children—would be unappreciative of rational principles of, for example, sound diet and, governed by unskilled bodily capacities such as the mouth watering, would be vulnerable to advertisements for junk food (464d–e). Socrates contrasts investigations of the body—which are unskilled, confused, lacking any distinction between what *seems* and what *is* good—with investigations of the soul—which are skillful, unconfused, and discriminating (465d–e). In the *Gorgias*, Socrates describes the bodily unskilled investigation as aiming at the pleasant while ignorant of the good (465a), while the soul's skilled investigation aims at the good. If I as an interpreter focus on one-sentence answers, I can cite this passage as evidence of conflict with claims made in the *Protagoras* about pleasure being the aim of the soul's metric art. But if I postulate that "pleasure" in this passage in the *Gorgias* means sensate pleasure, the contrast between bodily capacity and soul's skill can be seen as part of the same theory uncoiled in the argumentation of both dialogues.

In the *Protagoras*, we learn that each metric skill, in contrast to the bodily capacity, can do the following (356d7–e2):

*a*ʹ. Reveal truth (*dêlôsasa to alêthes*) to the soul. As astronomy can discover the true size and brightness of stars and sun, the art of the athletic trainer can reveal the harms and benefits, with associated pleasures and pains, of poor and good posture.

*b*ʹ. Keep the soul oriented to truth (*tên psuchên menousan epi tô*[*i*] *alêthei*). A trained athlete, for example, will correctly interpret the sensation of muscle burn, which can loom much larger, phenomenologically, as compared to twinges in joints. Whereas untrained athletes can find the experience of muscle burn sufficiently painful to stop exercising while not noticing joint twinges, trained athletes can come to enjoy muscle burn while carefully noticing joint twinges.

c′. Give the soul peace (*hêsuchian*). The fluctuations in perspective or circumstance are properly weighed; vacillation is eliminated.

d′. Dethrone appearance from rulership (*akuron an epoiêse to phantasma*) over the soul's choices and actions. The soul acts like a trained rather than an untrained athlete, with Mucius rather than Austin.

e′. Make life safe (*esôsen an ton bion*). I can understand the invulnerability in life and death that Socrates notoriously claims for the good man (*Ap.* 41d; see chapter 8).

I have described the analogies between sensations of objects of perception and of pleasure and pain. There are also disanalogies. Of particular interest is that the objects of perception may be susceptible to scales of measurement to which pleasures and pains are not. Thus Taylor (1991: 194) claims that measurements of sizes of perceptual objects do but measurements of sizes of pleasures and pains do not "involve the application of any quantitative scale." Since Socrates requires measurement of pleasures and pains, the disanalogy Taylor alleges would be crucial.

But Taylor is wrong. He assumes any quantitative measurement must involve a "numerically specifiable unit of measurement" (1991: 197; see also 198). Any *interval* scale of measurement does require a unit and origin: examples of such scales are centigrade or Fahrenheit scales of temperature measurement. But *ordinal* scales do not require units (or origin): an example is the scratch test for hardness of minerals. Measurements of pleasures and pains can be made on an ordinal scale: as Taylor himself admits, "We are quite happy to say that we enjoyed something more than we normally do, or less than someone else did" (1991: 198).[6]

Nonetheless, there is a disanalogy having to do with measurement: perceptions are susceptible to interval scales while pleasures and pains (as Socrates and ordinary language conceives them) are not. But this disanalogy is not crucial. For a reliable ordinal scale is all that Socrates requires for a metric skill that will keep our lives safe. And, though Socrates describes his own possession of the skill as "nothing to speak of" (*oligou tinos axia esti kai oudenos*, *Ap.* 23a7; see also 23b3–4, 20d6–9), even it is sufficient to demonstrate such things as that it is worse to corrupt the young than to benefit them (*Ap.* 25d–e), that it is worse to corrupt one's soul than one's body (*Cri.* 47d–48a), that it is more profitable to be just than unjust (*Rep.* I, 347e–354a; see chapter 8 of this book for defense of this argument), and that it is best neither to do nor suffer wrong, better to suffer than to do wrong, worse to do wrong and be punished for it, and worst of all to do wrong and escape punishment (*Grg.* 469b–479d). These results do demonstrate the possibility of the metric art in which Socrates would love to acquire significant expertise.[7]

What Does the Metric Art Measure?

The metric art has, I believe, been thought a technique for measuring magnitudes of sensations. On a physicalist reading the Socratic art would be perfected in a device that measures stimulations of pleasure and pain centers in the brain. Should it turn out that painful and pleasant sensations can be identified with such stimulations of the nervous system, then the measurement art would be perfected when we develop an instrument that measures the intensity and duration of electrical-chemical magnitudes carried by, let us say, the C-fibers, producing a meter reading on a dial. Certainly no signs of such a science are found or anticipated in the Socratic dialogues. If the Socratic art identifies pleasures and pains with the raw feel of sensations accompanying bodily, aesthetic, or intellectual activities, then the measurement art would have to do with techniques of phenomenological introspection and graphic description. Again, there are no signs of Socrates using such procedures in the dialogues. On the contrary, as shown above, Socrates recommends against such reliance on the authority of subjective appearances in the *Protagoras* and derides the graphic descriptions of torture that weigh heavily on Polus's mind. In any case, ordinary Greek usage lends little support to such physicalist or phenomenological interpretations of the Greek plural "pleasures" used in the *Protagoras*.[8]

Taylor (1991: 196) is unable to find any instances of the metric art displayed, however inexpertly, in Socratic dialogues. Irwin (1995: 85 and 111–113) believes it possible that such a metric art might promote the virtues of bravery or temperance but certainly not justice. Perhaps both are assuming that the metric art is a technique for measuring magnitudes of sensate pleasures rather than modal pleasures. But it is my view that the point of dialectical examination—the metric art—is not to calculate magnitudes of present or future sensations. It is my view that dialectic, on the one hand, and pleasure/pain sensations, on the other, are two ways, superior and inferior, of measuring the very same thing: the magnitude of goodness, which is modal pleasure. Either way can be used for investigating immediate or future pleasures and pains (see *Grg.* 465d-e).

My hypothesis is that the art that Socrates describes as the salvation of human life in the *Protagoras*, the technique for weighing activities against each other, determines what provides the greatest magnitude of what all humans desire. Socrates identifies this object as "pleasure" or "living well" in the *Protagoras*; "living well" or "happiness" in the *Euthydemus*; "living well," "living blessedly," "living happily," and "living profitably" in the *Republic*; "living well," "living admirably," and "living righteously" in the *Crito*; and "doing well" and "being happy" in the *Charmides*. My hypothesis is that the measuring art that saves our lives in the *Protagoras* is the same art Socrates identifies as the wisdom which only the gods possess in the *Apology*, and as the knowledge of what is good and evil in the *Charmides* and *Laches*. It is the art that educates and improves us, making us admirable and good, with souls as good as possible, giving us the most valuable thing, virtue (*Ap.* 20b1, 24e4–5, 25a9–10, 29e1– 2, 30a1, 31b5). It is this metric art that justifies Socrates' famous use of the craft analogy in his examinations of virtue—what it is—in many passages.

On my interpretation the metric art is a technique for weighing one activity against another. The Socratic art would accordingly be perfected in techniques for weighing activities against each other. There are many examples of this in Socratic texts. I have mentioned *Apology* 25d–e, *Crito* 47d–48a, *Republic* I 347e–354a, and *Gorgias* 469b–479d above. Moreover, in the *Apology* Socrates weighs a life of philosophizing against non-philosophizing (28b–29d). He weighs appealing to the sympathies of the jurors against appealing only to their reason (34c–35d). He weighs the appropriate penalty he should propose to the jury after his conviction (36b–38b). In the *Crito*, Socrates uses his dialectic to weigh the action of remaining in prison against the action of running away (46c–54e). In the *Euthydemus* he weighs *possession* against *use* of goods (280b–d) and knowledgeable against unknowledgeable use (280e–281d).

The Metaphor of Weight Measurement in Socratic Dialogues

The language of measurement, in particular of weight, as it occurs in Socratic dialogues is consistent with my hypothesis. Socrates speaks of measuring by a yardstick how well a youth has turned out (*stathmêton*, *Chrm.* 154b8) and what a person says (*stathmai*, *Lys.* 205a3), as well as pleasures (*stathmômenon*, *Grg.* 465d3). There is no mention of the balance beam (*zugos*), apart from *Protagoras* 356b2, in the Socratic dialogues, but in *Republic* VIII (550e7) Socrates says that virtue and wealth are so opposed that if they were set on the scales of a balance beam (*en plastiggi zugou*), they would always incline in opposite directions. However, when I consider the occurrences of the cognates of the adjective *axios*, "weighing as much," I find that the language of weighted measurement and comparison occurs frequently throughout Socrates' and ordinary Greek word usage.[9]

Socrates asserts in the *Apology* that his principal reproach to others is that they attach "greatest weight (*ta pleistou axia*) to the least things and worthless weight (*ta phaulotera*) to the greatest things" (30a1–2). The *Protagoras* explains why this is so: they are ignorant of the metric art that would show them the correct weights. Socrates, insignificant though his own knowledge is, confidently asserts in the *Crito* what it is that has the greatest weight: "virtue and justice weigh the most (*pleistou axion*) for human beings" (53c7). Unfortunately, people because of their ignorance are hoodwinked by flattering pseudo-sciences like rhetoric, which only "seem to weigh the most" (*dokei pleistou axia einai*, *Grg.* 464d3). These passages indicate that the wisdom Socrates values, which is the virtue he seeks, will keep souls safe by measuring and determining the correct weights to attach to justice, power, wealth, life, and the like. On my interpretation there is one coherent position underlying all these assertions.

Does Socrates Consistently Seek to Maximize or Optimize Goods and Pleasures?

For *maximizers*, more is always better; for *optimizers*, more is not always better.[10] In *Republic* I, Thrasymachus praises maximization (*pleonexia*) as a life plan; in opposition, Socrates holds that there is an optimal mean between excess and defect in every wise choice and that only the ignorant choose to have more and more (349e–350a). In the *Gorgias*, Callicles asserts that the best life will be a life where one satisfies the largest possible appetites (491e–492a); Socrates opposes this maximization plan with the optimization thesis that the best life consists in self-restraint and moderation (492d–494a). So *Republic* I and the *Gorgias* contain a consistent one-sentence answer: Socrates is an optimizer. But the *Protagoras* contains a conflicting one-sentence answer. In that dialogue Socrates maintains a maximization thesis: the wise choice will be for the maximum amount of pleasure (356b–e). Now on my interpretation of the *Protagoras*, Socrates seeks to maximize not sensations of pleasure but types of activity. Accordingly Socrates' maximization thesis in the *Protagoras* can be harmonized with the optimization or "mean" thesis of *Republic* I and the *Gorgias*. For, with Aristotle, Socrates can claim that "the mean is in a way an extreme" (*NE* II.6 1107a23): "virtue is a mean in respect of its substance [that is, neither too much nor too little food, strings neither too tight nor too loose (examples taken from *Rep.* I 349e–350a), shoes neither too big nor too little, neither too many nor too few (example from *Grg.* 490e)] and in respect of its definition [a mean between excess and deficiency, *Rep.* I 350a], but with respect to excellence and rightness it is an extreme" (*NE* II.6 1107a6–7)—the best action and life is the most excellent and the most righteous.

Comparison of Socrates' Representational View to Modern Hedonism

As I interpret Socrates, he understands bodily sensations of pleasure and pain as by their nature representations, albeit imperfect, of benefits and harms. It is as such representations of value that sensations acquire whatever value they may have. For modern hedonism (see for example Hume's *Treatise* II part 3 section 3) as for Goldstein, any representational power of such sensations is irrelevant to their value; intrinsically they possess obvious goodness and badness.

For both Socratic and modern hedonism, calculation of magnitudes of good and bad is the ultimate human wisdom (and in this respect Nussbaum 1986 is justified in quoting Bentham in the epigraph to her chapter on the *Protagoras*: "Every circumstance by which the condition of an individual can be influenced, being remarked and inventoried, nothing . . . [is] left to chance, caprice, or unguided discretion, everything being surveyed and set down in dimension, number, weight, and measure"). But the calculations of the Socratic and modern are radically different. For the modern hedonist, the bodily sensations are the ultimate constituents—the atoms or quanta, as it were—of value. For the Socratic hedonist, bodily sensations are not identified with but merely represent objects or activities that constitute value. And bodily sensations are imperfect as representations—misleading, disorienting, vacillating, unsafe. A metric skill would provide perfect representations—true, oriented, constant, safe. Bodily sensations, rather than being the atoms of value, are mere *phantasmata* that must be "dethroned from authority" (*Prt.* 356d–e). In regard to the modern hedonist, Socrates might well adopt the terminology of the *Republic* (V 476c): like the lover of sights and sounds, the modern hedonist, thinking that pleasure sensations are themselves worthy of pursuit, confuses what *resembles* for what *is*. (Socrates' description of pleasure and pain sensations as mixed up with each other, at *Pho.* 60b and *Grg.* 496e, is extended by Plato to qualities of sensible objects in general at *Rep.* V 479a–c.) In this respect—in regard to that about which the calculation is—it is highly misleading to quote Bentham as an epigraph to an account of Socrates' hedonism. If I confuse Benthamite with Socratic calculation, I, finding no hint of a Benthamite operation anywhere in the Socratic texts and ignoring the omnipresent dialectical weighing, might very well complain with Taylor (1991: 196) of this defect in the *Protagoras*, that it requires an unfulfilled project.

Comparison of Socrates' Representational View
to Kraut's Account

Kraut (1994: 46) believes that felt pain "normally accompanies" an injury or interruption of healthy processes. On Socrates' account, there is a stronger connection. Felt pain is not a mere accompaniment but an (imperfect) representation of harm. Kraut allows sense pain to have extrinsic negative value: it can distract us from good activities or objects for us as human beings. On Socrates' account, the distracting power of pain might be good or bad for us as human beings, depending on whether the representation is true or false. Even if the representation is true, whether its distracting power is good will depend on the metric art's determination of what weight the represented benefit or harm has in the circumstances. To illuminate the lack of intrinsic value in pleasure or pain, Kraut gives parallel cases of unpleasant but not physically painful odors and sounds, claiming that they are not bad apart from the distractions they might bring. On Socrates' account, the distracting power of the foul smell or grating noise might be good or bad for us as human beings, depending on whether the representation is true or false, and if true, depending on the metric art's determination of what weight the bodily good or bad has in the circumstances.

Kraut's account, according to which there is no intrinsic value to the sensations themselves of pleasure or pain (as opposed to possibly associated benefits or harms) is vulnerable to Goldstein's objection: Kraut leaves it a mystery how it is that pain sensations came to be correlated with harm in the first place. The Socratic account can explain the correlation: it is the nature of pain sensations to represent physical harms that are pains, just as it is the nature of sensations of vision to represent physical objects that are visible. Both vision's correlation with visible objects and pain's correlation with painful objects are to be explained by one's theory of perception. I do not claim that there are no mysteries involved in perception, but they at any rate will be equally shared by the competing accounts of pleasure and pain as intrinsically or not intrinsically valuable.

Comparison of the Representational View
to Goldstein's View

Goldstein (1989: 258) holds that "pain's educative and protective powers originate from its intrinsic badness." To attribute intrinsic badness to sensations of pain makes it impossible to explain the role our understanding has in mitigating, eliminating, or even taking pleasure in what can seem a painful sensation. For, as noticed before, untrained athletes may be strongly averse to the strong sensation of "burning" in a muscle group being exercised but notice little or nothing painful in slight twinges in joints. After training, athletes tolerate or even enjoy the burning but are strongly averse to joint twinges. If there is intrinsic bad in sensations, then the same sensation (burning or twinging) mysteriously acquires or loses this badness after training. Better to say with Socrates that pain's protective powers originate from its representational power (*hê tou phainomenou dunamis*) of receiving impressions, though such protection is often disoriented and unsafe.

Sensations of pain, when understood as by their nature representations of harms, will lead us to define pain in terms of harm. Likewise pleasure will be defined in terms of benefit. Whereas traditional hedonism has been understood as a reduction of value to sensation, Socratic hedonism is a reduction of sensation to value. While he is not necessarily a hedonist, Goldstein's statements of the obvious badness of pain (and goodness of pleasure) suggest a reduction of value to sensation along the lines of traditional hedonism, in contrast to Socratic hedonism.

7.5 Conclusion

On Kraut's account, the sensations of pleasure and pain are non-representational and possess no intrinsic value. Yet they are correlated with value, and the explanation of that correlation is a mystery. On Goldstein's account, the sensations themselves of pleasure and pain are also non-representational but possess intrinsic value. Yet the brute fact of their intrinsic value is a mystery. On a representational account, the sensations, like any experience that is a representation, are actualizations of a human capacity and as such may have intrinsic value. Let me elaborate.

Actualizations of human capacities, which may in a broad sense be called activities, have intrinsic value when undergone or performed for their own sake, extrinsic value when undergone or performed for the sake of something else.[11] When one weaves only for the sake of the cloth to wear or sell, the weaving has no intrinsic value; when one weaves not out of necessity but as a leisure activity, and not as a recreation (which is done for the sake of stress reduction or recuperation) but as an expression of one's nature, then the activity of weaving has intrinsic value for one and is in fact a pleasure (a modal pleasure, not necessarily a sense pleasure; see chapters 6 and 10 of this book).

The same can be said for the animal capacity for vision. When one's vision is only put to use to find something, as when hunting through drain sludge to find a lost ring, then that activity of vision has no intrinsic value.

But when the looking is done for its own sake, as when stopping at a road-side scenic overlook, then the activity has intrinsic value and is a modal pleasure.

Nearly the same holds true for sensations of pleasure and pain. When put to use for the sake of something else, they have, as activities in the broad sense, extrinsic value. In the case of sensations of pleasure, this can happen when a pastry chef taste-tests a recipe; in the case of pain, when a patient in recovery tests the range of motion of an injured limb. And sensations of pleasure have intrinsic value when undergone for their own sake, as when a gourmet enjoys a pastry at the end of a meal. (Such cases are quite common but not necessary for pleasure. For sensations of pleasure are many times irrelevant to the value of an activity, as for example in sports players: golfers might well not golf for any particular sensation of pleasure.) On the other hand, cases where sensations of pain are pursued for their own sake are rare or non-existent. Some cases that come to mind—masochists and hyper-sophisticated aesthetes—should be analyzed, I believe, following Goldstein (1983: 219–223 and 1980: 351): on close examination, pains for such people appear to be pursued for extrinsic goals such as a need for punishment (the masochist) or to heighten a sense of relief (one who waits before scratching the itch) or to contribute to the overall balance of an experience (one who leaves one mosquito bite unscratched for a more refined experience of the relief of scratching). On the other hand, the activity of such sensation could conceivably have intrinsic value to a lover of experience per se. If such lovers exist, they could value painful sensations not only for extrinsic reasons such as educational value but also intrinsically as fulfilling their natures as indiscriminate lovers of experiences.

In the last three paragraphs, I have spoken of positive intrinsic and extrinsic values. Similar remarks can be made for negative intrinsic and extrinsic values, which activities in the broad sense have when they are avoided (rather than done or undergone) for their own sake or for the sake of something else.

The intrinsic value in all of the above cases turns out to be in their modal rather than sensory aspect, that is, as actualizing a human capacity rather than as raw qualitative experience. For the value is indicated not by the particular character of a qualitative feeling, but the motive (which itself depends on the nature or character) of the one engaging in the activity. And the value is best explained not as a brute fact of the qualitative experience but by understanding the activity as expressing and completing (in the case of positive value; distorting and frustrating in the case of negative value) the nature of the agent as, in our examples, a weaver or perceiver. In the case of representational experience—whether the representation is through vision, pleasure, or pain—the activity may be connected to the human function as rational animal. Both vision and pleasure play roles—which are often played for their own sake—in our theoretical (cognitive, including evaluative) grasp of the world, and also in our practical exercise of our capacities in the world.

On my account, therefore, there is possible intrinsic value to sense pleasure and pain, though not of the sort found in traditional hedonism and Goldstein's account. I have ascribed a modal hedonism to Socrates (in chapter 6) and in this chapter have identified that hedonism with Socrates' metric hedonism of the *Protagoras*, which makes virtue a matter of knowledge. (I cannot here discuss the problems arising from Socrates' identification of virtue with knowledge.) My aim in this chapter has been to give a compelling account of the value of modal as opposed to sensate pleasure for a human being. For it is modal hedonism that reconciles Socrates the hedonist with Socrates the virtue supremacist (as shown in chapter 10).

EIGHT

The Righteous Are Happy

In the first book of Plato's *Republic* the character Thrasymachus presents Socrates with the immoralist's challenge. The immoralist notes that the consequences of being moral (or *righteous*)[1] can be disastrous for one's happiness, consequences such as the horrors of imprisonment, torture, and death. By contrast, the intended consequences of immorality are highly desired components of happiness, such as power, wealth, and honor (343a–344c). Therefore morality is a bad life-style for a human being, and moral people must be simpleminded; they cannot be wise (348b–d).

Socrates, in response, leads Thrasymachus to the conclusion that unrighteousness is never more profitable than righteousness (354a). That conclusion is a corollary of an argument that the righteous are happy and the unrighteous miserable (352b–354a), which in turn depends on the lemma that righteousness is excellence and wisdom, and unrighteousness defect and foolishness (349a–350d). This argument provides the cornerstone of Socratic ethics. It allows us to understand Socrates' claim that virtue is sufficient for happiness, that nothing bad can happen to a good man (*Ap.* 41d1). Such understanding can cause a fundamental change in one's life. In addition, this argument establishes that righteousness, that is, virtue, is the excellence of the human soul (see premise 19 below). This result is crucial to the scholarly goal of this book, which is a reconciliation of Socrates the hedonist and Socrates the virtue supremacist, because it will allow Socrates to say that virtuous activity is one and the same as true pleasure for a human being (see chapter 10).

The scholars who have examined the soundness of Socrates' argument for the foundations of his ethics by and large disagree with the Delphic oracle, which pronounced Socrates the wisest of men (*Ap.* 21a). They by and large disagree with Alcibiades' assessment of Socratic argument as godlike (*Symp.* 222a3; see also 216e7). For they by and large see his argument as more laughable than godlike.[2] In this chapter I defend the assessment of the oracle and Alcibiades; I argue that it is a sound argument. I shall begin by defending the lemma. After stating each premise I shall clarify its terms and argue for its truth. As each inference is made, I shall defend its validity. Then I shall do the same for the argument proper. The corollary will be obvious.

For ease of exposition, I have reordered the premises from what is found in the text. Since many of the standard objections that occur to readers take the form that Socrates is equivocating in one way or another, I have found it necessary to ignore the suggestively embroidered meaning of many of the premises. While my focus on but a few main threads of the argument has the advantage of answering the charge of equivocation, it has the disadvantage of giving a threadbare interpretation.[3] Again, the brachylogies of the text have encouraged other objections. My remedy, an expanded style and notation, comes at the cost of some elegance. Finally, my view (see section 5.1 of this book) is that Socrates in his conversations aims not at the logical goal of sound argument, nor the sophistical goal of ad hominem persuasion, but at the pedagogical goal of understanding. However, in this case as so often, the logical goal is close enough to the pedagogical goal that it is convenient to treat him as engaged in constructing logically sound arguments, according to the conventions of analytic philosophy.

8.1 Lemma that Righteousness Is Excellence

Premise 1 Is True

The text suggests the following.

1.   The knowledgeable man attempts (in his actions as such) to have more than his contradictory (that is, anyone ignorant) but not more than his counterpart (that is, anyone knowledgeable), whereas the ignorant man attempts (in

his actions as such) to have more than both his contradictory and his coun-terpart (350a6–b2).[4]

The idea is that the knowledgeable are *optimizers* while the ignorant are *maximizers*.[5] Let me first make precise the idea that the knowledge-able are optimizers. Let *S* be or be like a skill, and *O* the object of the deliberate action determined by the person knowledgeable in *S*.

1*a*. The man knowledgeable in *S* attempts (in his actions as such) to possess a superior quantity of *O* relative to his contradictory (that is, anyone ignorant of *S*) but not relative to his counterpart (that is, anyone knowledgeable in *S*).

Socrates' own examples will illustrate: the musician tuning a lyre at 349e10–15 and the physician prescribing a patient's diet at 350a1–4.

What is it that the expert tuner, *harmottomenos luran* ("tuning the lyre," 349e10–11), attempts to have more of than one ignorant of tuning, but not more of than the other expert tuners? His action here is *harmottesthai* ("to get in tune"); the object of that action is *harmonia* ("tunedness"). The superior quantity (which is attempted relative to the non-musician but not relative to the expert musician) therefore is of *harmonia*.

Notice that in English we may speak of student musicians in compe-titions being judged, among other things, by the superiority of the into-nation that they may or may not possess in playing or, conceivably, tun-ing their instruments. Violinists, for example, need by tightening or loosening their strings to reproduce the note *A* (heard from an external source) on their third string, and then to produce a *D* on their second string (again, by tightening or loosening it) by adjusting it to sound a fifth on the diatonic scale when played as a chord with the *A* string. This takes skill, and one might imagine a group of student violinists being judged in their ability to tune their instruments as part of a competition.

Notice also—this is something Socrates means to draw attention to—that *having superior intonation* does not mean *having tighter* (*or looser*) *strings*; for if so, the best intonation would be had by the student who had the tightest (or loosest) strings. One might say that the degree of intonation supervenes on the degree of tension of the strings, but intonation and tight-ness are not the same.[6] Plato might say that strings by being tightened come to participate in the Form Harmony.

What is the *ti* ("something," 350a1) that the expert physician, *en tê(i) edôdê(i) ê posei* ("in [prescribing] food or drink," 350a1), attempts to have more of than the non-physician, but not more of than the other expert physicians? It will depend on what verb is supplied with the *en tê(i) edôdê(i) ê posei*. Exactly which verb is not important. Suppose it is *nemein* ("to prescribe," used at *Grg.* 490c2). The objects of *nemein* are *nomoi* ("prescriptions"), and in the case of a physician's *nemein* presumably the objects are *hugieinoi nomoi* ("healing prescriptions," that is, a healing course of treatment). Thus one should take the superior quantity (which is attempted relative to the non-physician but not relative to the other expert physicians) to be of *hugieinoi nomoi*. I take it that the physician does attempt to have a more healing course of treatment than the non-physician in the food or drink prescribed for an illness.[7] As before, *having a more healing prescription* does not mean *having more food or drink in the prescription*.

The examples of the musician and physician are meant to illustrate the truth of premise 1*a*. But it might appear that counter-examples to 1*a* can be produced. In particular, it might seem that there are cases of people knowledgeable in a skill who, contrary to the claim of 1*a*, attempt to have more than each other. For instance, it might seem that this happens in the case of competitive skills, such as generalship or boxing.[8] Let me sharpen this objection by noting that practically any skill can become competitive. Thus we might make this objection in terms of Socrates' own examples, the musician tuning a lyre and the physician prescribing a patient's diet.

Musicians in competitions are typically judged, among other things, by the superiority of the intonation they may or may not possess in playing, but let me conceive of a competition to judge the superiority of the intonation they may or may not possess merely in tuning their instruments. Let me, accordingly, imagine musicians competing with each other, where winning the competition consists in possessing better intonation than the rest as the result of tuning the lyre. And the point of the objection, which is certainly true, is that, though they compete, they nonetheless remain practitioners of a skill.

This objection is disarmed by a precise use of *skill words* (that is, names of skills or the adjectivals or personal substantives derived from those names, as for example *musical* and *musician* are derived from *music*). By the way, this use will accord with the precision of Thrasymachus (at 340d2–e6), before the start of Socrates' argument. A skill comprises many different aspects, each of which may be possessed to one degree or another.

Now I may reconsider the objection. The point made in the objection was that a musician (in the ordinary way of speaking) might compete against and thus try to have more (sc. superiority of intonation) than other musicians (in the ordinary sense). But, taking the argument's use of skill words in the precise sense, the objection can no longer be made. For let *intonation* be one aspect of music, and let *being in tune* (as opposed to being to some degree flat or sharp) *in one's instrument* be the degree of that aspect which may be possessed by the tuner. Now it is only insofar as rivals fail to sound the proper note (by possessing in some degree a flat or sharp instrument) that the competitor attempts to have more; thus it is only insofar as rivals are non-musical (in that aspect, to that degree) that the competitor attempts to have more than they. It would be absurd for her as a musician (in that aspect, to that degree) to attempt to have superiority of intonation over a correctly tuned string, that is, a string tuned by another musician (in that aspect, to that degree).

The same defense of Socrates' argument could be made in the case of competing physicians. Presumably, in such a competition, the winner would be the one who produced and possessed the most healing prescription of diet. It is true that physicians (in the ordinary sense) conceivably might compete against and thus try to have a more healing prescription than other physicians (in the ordinary sense). But, taking the argument's use of skill words in the precise sense, the objection no longer holds. For let *prescribing diet* be the relevant aspect of the physician's skill, and let *dispensing the right degree of food and drink* (as opposed to too little or too much) *in one's prescription* be the relevant degree of that aspect which may be possessed by the physician; the rest is obvious.

Can such a defense of Socrates' argument be made in the case of the examples of generalship and boxing? In the expert opinion of N. B. Forrest, winning the battle for the general consists in getting there "firstest with the mostest." This might seem to make generalship a *pleonectic* skill (that is, a skill where the knowledgeable man attempts to have more than both his contradictory and his counterpart; see n. 9), since there seems no limit on the "more" the general would desire: get to the battleground *as soon as* possible with the *most* force. But even this gross simplification of the skill shows the need for balance, not excess; for optimizing, not maximizing. For considerations of speed of action mitigate considerations of force, and there will be a best balance of those considerations in any given situation. Thus, a general who is expert (in those aspects, to the right degrees) will attempt to achieve that balance, not exceed it, and thus will attempt to have more (sc. superiority in time and force) than the non-expert (in those aspects, to those degrees) but not more than the expert (in those aspects, to those degrees). The same sort of answer applies as well to boxing. I take this discussion to indicate that no counter-examples to Socrates' premise that the knowledgeable are optimizers, made precise in statement 1*a*, can be found, and hence that it is true.

Let me next make precise the idea that the ignorant are maximizers. Recall that in the case of optimizers I referred to the object of a deliberate action, an object that is identified by some skill or knowledge. But in the case of ignorance, the object of a deliberate action may have no such coherent identity. In the case of ignorance of some skill, the identity of the object of its (the ignorance's) deliberate actions may be incoherent in the following way. The person who deliberately acts with the object of some skill, but whose deliberation is ignorant, might confuse that object with something else. For example, if I wanted to tune a string of a lyre, but ignorantly confused the object of the string-tuning skill (that is, a tuned string) with something else (say, a tight string), then the identity of the object of my action is incoherent in that it is both the same as the object of the knowledgeable action (that is, a tuned string) and different from the object of the knowledgeable action (for I aim at a tight string). My ignorant action in a sense has an object, but its identity is incoherent in that I see no difference between *tight* and *in tune*. Now let O' be the confused object of the deliberate action determined by the person ignorant of S. I may then make precise the idea that the ignorant are maximizers as follows:

1b. The man ignorant of S attempts (in his actions as such) to possess a superior quantity of O' relative to his contradictory (that is, anyone knowledgeable in S) and to his counterpart (that is, anyone ignorant of S).

Let me consider now the truth of premise 1*b* in the light of Socrates' examples. If the skill is string tuning, one who is ignorant of this skill (in one's actions as such) might aim at some object that confuses tuned strings (the object of tuning) with some other object, say, tight strings. Why does such a one attempt to have more of this object than everyone, both those knowledgeable and those ignorant of string tuning?

Ignorance of string tuning is insufficient to cause ignorant string-tuning action. Also necessary is desire for tuned strings. Knowledge of string tuning likewise requires desire for tuned strings in order to cause string-tuning action. Desire, ignorant or knowledgeable, continues (absent intervening factors) until it finds satisfaction by achieving its object. But knowledgeable desire has a clear object, here, tuned strings, unconfused with such things as tight strings. Thus knowledgeable desire will be sated with tuned strings and will cease to cause further string-tuning action. But ignorant desire has its object, tuned strings, confused with tight strings. Since strings can be ever more tightly tuned, there is no point at which ignorant desire is sated and ceases to cause further string-tuning action. The ignorant human being sees no difference between tighter and more in tune; hence the desire-triggered action has no clear end; hence such a one has pleonexia.[9]

The case of ignorant confusion of tuned strings with tight strings illustrates premise 1*b*. Now I can generalize. Whenever the end of the ignorant action is confused with something of which, by its nature, more and more can indefinitely be acquired, premise 1*b* will be true. But every skill's object is a mean between more and less, and anyone who fails to confuse the mean with more or less is not ignorant.[10] Thus premise 1*b* is true.

Premise 2 Is True

The text suggests the following.

2. The righteous man attempts (in his actions as such) to have more than his contradictory (that is, anyone unrighteous) but not more than his counterpart (that is, anyone righteous), whereas the unrighteous man attempts (in his actions as such) to have more than both his contradictory and his counterpart (349c11–d2).

As with premise 1, this premise contains two ideas: the righteous optimize; the unrighteous maximize. More precisely, let O be the object of the deliberate action determined by the righteous man, and O' the object of the deliberate action determined by the unrighteous man. Then:

2*a*. The righteous man attempts to possess a superior quantity of O relative to his contradictory (that is, anyone unrighteous) but not relative to his counterpart (that is, anyone righteous).

2*b*. The unrighteous man attempts to possess a superior quantity of O' relative to both his contradictory (that is, anyone righteous) and his counterpart (that is, anyone unrighteous).

Since it is a matter of dispute between Socrates and Thrasymachus whether it is the righteous or unrighteous man who is or is like the knowledgeable man, it would be a mistake to interpret O on the basis of a verbal similarity to the knowledgeable man in the following manner:

What is it that the righteous man wants to have more of than an unrighteous man, but not more of than a righteous man? His action is *dikaioun* ("to set right"); the object of that action is *dikaiosunê* ("righteousness"). The superior quantity (which is desired relative to the unrighteous but not relative to the righteous man) therefore is of *dikaiosunê*.

For to read the argument in that way is to read it as begging the question against Thrasymachus: the unrighteous man's object would be implied to be a confusion of *dikaiosunê* and something else.[11] Likewise it would be begging the question to assume that the unrighteous man has the clear object, *adikia* ("unrighteousness"), and the righteous man is the one with the confused end.

It is possible to interpret O and O' in a way that will not beg the question. Socrates and Thrasymachus agree that both the unrighteous and the righteous man are concerned as such with the conduct not of parts of human life, such as musical or medical activity, but of human life *as a whole* (*holou biou diagôgên*, 344e1–2). Socrates will even agree to Thrasymachus's characterization of the goal in terms of "profiting" (*lusiteloun*, 344e2–3).[12] Socrates believes that the unrighteous man is ignorant about how human life as a whole is most profitable, that such a man confuses the possession of profit with the possession of the most wealth or power. Conversely Thrasymachus believes it is not a confusion to identify greatest profit with greatest material wealth or power; rather, that the righteous man is confused in identifying fair play (or whatever is seen as righteous) with the superior conduct of one's own life as a whole. Since Socrates and Thrasymachus agree that the object of both the righteous and the unrighteous man in their deliberate actions as such is *superior conduct or profit in human life as a whole,* I let this be O and O', but so as not to beg the question either way, I leave open which of O and O' clearly is this object and which is this object only in a confused way.[13]

Are Socrates and Thrasymachus right that both the righteous and unrighteous man as such attempt to possess profit in human life as a whole? It is possible to object that this agreement confuses moral with prudent activity.[14] It seems easy enough to imagine cases where the action dictated by selfish considerations of prudence is at variance with the moral action. Those cases would show that *profitable human life as a whole* is ambiguous between the morally superior life and the prudentially advantageous life.

A precise use of *righteous* and *profit in human life as a whole* disarms this objection. In cases where there seems to be variance between dictates of prudence and morality, there are those who do the righteous act. Among those who do the righteous act, some would believe that their righteous act is not prudentially most advantageous in the circumstances, while others would believe that their righteous act is also prudentially most advantageous in the circumstances (Socrates in the *Crito* is a notorious example). I will call *righteous* only the second sort of person, the one who invariably sees the concerns of morality as unsurpassable grounds for prudential advantage.

This sense of *righteous,* so long as I keep it throughout the argument, will cause no fallacy of equivocation. Nor is it at variance with some of the most influential sources of the use of *righteous* in our culture. It is likely that Jesus, for example, has often been understood to be pointing out that

considerations of morality are unsurpassable grounds for prudential advantage in his rhetorical question, "What shall it profit a man, if he shall
gain the whole world, and lose his own soul?"[15] Moreover, let *profit in human
life as a whole* mean, precisely, the object of prudential deliberation, which
I have imagined, in developing my objection, to be sometimes at variance with the object of moral deliberation.

How do these senses of *righteous* and *profit in human life as a whole* avoid
the objection? The objection was that Socrates and Thrasymachus, in
agreeing that both the righteous and unrighteous man as such attempt to
possess profit in human life as a whole, were confusing morality and prudence. But, in this sense of *righteous*, neither one is confused. Socrates is
not confused, because he means to defend the claim that the unrighteous
man is ignorant about how human life as a whole is most profitable, and
that the righteous man is correct in understanding that the considerations
of morality are unsurpassably prudent. If I make this objection, it does
not show that Socrates' argument is fallacious; it shows rather that I
side with Thrasymachus in the argument. For I would believe, with
Thrasymachus, that the righteous man is confused in identifying moral
conduct with superior conduct of one's own life as a whole. For I would
believe that sometimes these are at odds with each other. I would think,
with Thrasymachus, that the righteous man, in this sense of *righteous*,
attempts to have profit in human life as a whole, but that this is the object of his action only in a confused way. I would hold, with Thrasymachus,
that prudence is different from righteousness and that prudence apart from
righteousness clearly, not confusedly, has as its object profit in human life
as a whole.

The argument requires of premise 2 that, first, both righteous and
unrighteous action attempt to have profit in human life as a whole; that,
second, one action clearly has it as object while the other has it as object
only in a confused way; and that, third, premise 2, on pain of begging the
question, must not specify which action has the end in a clear way and
which has it in a confused way. Now according to my interpretation of *O*
and *O´*, and according to the sense I have given to *righteous* and *profit in
human life as a whole*, premises 2a and 2b, and hence premise 2, meet all of
these requirements.

Having established that premises *2a* and *2b* neither beg the question
against Thrasymachus nor fallaciously equivocate, let me now consider
their truth. On my reading of premise *2a*, the righteous man's object *O*
(which he may or may not be confusing with something else) is a prudentially good life. I take it as uncontroversial that he will attempt to have
more of this—more goodness or profit in human life—than the unrighteous man (though perhaps it is only ignorance that leads him to this at

tempt), but not more than a righteous man.[16] And on my reading of premise 2*b*, the unrighteous man's object *O'* (which he may or may not be confusing with something else) is also a prudentially good life. And I take it as uncontroversial that he will attempt to have more of this than everyone else, righteous or unrighteous. So both premises 2*a* and 2*b* are true.

Premise 3 Is True

The text suggests the following.

3. The knowledgeable man is wise and good (whereas the ignorant man is foolish and bad, 350b3–6).

This premise is uncontroversial, when interpreted as follows. Let *S* be or be like a skill.

3*a*. The man knowledgeable in *S* is wise and good in his *S* actions.
3*b*. The man ignorant of *S* is foolish and bad in his *S* actions.[17]

Premise 4 Is True

The text suggests the following.

4. Each of these (that is, the righteous man and the unrighteous man) is such as those who he is like (that is, either the knowledgeable and good or the ignorant and bad man, 349d10–11).

Premise 4 is often interpreted, uncharitably, as making the false claim that things alike in any one respect are alike in all respects.[18] A more charitable interpretation has the text stating the methodological rule for appraising analogical arguments.[19] This can be done by giving the following interpretation of the terms *is such as* and *is like*.

Is such as. Let *F* and *G* be adjectivals. Then an *F* man *is such as* a *G* man just in case the *F* man is *G*.

Is like. Let *F* and *G* be adjectivals. Then an *F* man *is like* a *G* man just in case there is a relevant respect *R* in which they are the same. *R* is *relevant* just in case it provides a connection being *F* and being *G*. *F* and *G* are *connected* just in case one can logically or causally infer that the *F* man is *G* and the *G* man is *F*. For example, being wise at string tuning is like being good at string tuning. For let *R* be *being able to tune strings well*. Then both being wise at string tuning and being good at string tuning are the same with respect to *R*. For both he who is wise and he who is good at string tuning are able to tune strings well. And R is relevant. For a man's goodness at string tuning is connected to his ability to tune strings well (for one can infer that a good string tuner is able to tune strings well, and that he who is able to tune strings well is a good string tuner), and that ability of his is connected to his wisdom at string tuning (for one can infer that he who is able to tune strings well is wise at string tuning, and that the wise string tuner is able to tune strings well).

On this interpretation, premise 4 is true. Let F and G be adjectivals. I need to show that if the F man is like the G man, then the F man is such as the G man. So let me suppose that the F man is like the G man. Then there is a relevant respect R in which the F man and the G man are the same. Since R is relevant, it connects being F and being G. But if there is a connection between being F and being G, I can infer that the F man will be G. So the F man is G. It follows that the F man is such as the G man; hence premise 4 is true.

From premises 1 and 3 it obviously follows that:

5. The wise and good man attempts (in his actions as such) to have more than his contradictory but not more than his counterpart, whereas the foolish and bad man attempts (in his actions as such) to have more than both his contradictory and his counterpart (350b7–12).

From premises 2 and 5 it follows that:

6. The righteous man is like the wise and good man, whereas the unrighteous man is like the foolish and bad man (350c4–5).

The inference from premises 2 and 5 to 6 is less than obvious.[20] Premises 2 and 5 establish a respect in which the righteous man and the wise and good man are the same, namely, attempting (in their actions as such) to have more than the contradictory but not more than the counterpart. Call this respect R. Premises 2 and 5 also establish a respect in which the unrighteous man and the foolish and bad man are the same, namely, in their pleonexia. Call this respect R'. I need to show that these two shared respects are relevant. This can be done by recalling and elaborating my defense of premise 1b.

The key is that desire is essential to deliberate action. Desire, ignorant or knowledgeable, continues (absent intervening factors) until and only until it finds satisfaction by achieving its object. Now knowledgeable desire has a clear object (for example tuned strings, unconfused with such things as tight strings). Thus knowledgeable and only knowledgeable desire will be sated with tuned strings and will cease to cause further string-tuning action. But ignorant desire has a confused object (for example, tuned strings are confused with tight strings). Since every skill's object is a mean between more and less, and anyone who fails to confuse the mean with more or less is not ignorant, there is no point at which ignorant desire is sated and ceases to cause further string-tuning action. The man ignorant about a given activity, who is the foolish and bad man with respect to that activity, sees no difference between, say, tighter and more in tune, and thus his desire-triggered action has no clear end, and thus the ignorant and only the ignorant man has pleonexia. Thus there is a connection between R and wisdom and goodness in a given activity (for the knowledgeable is the wise and good man in a given activity), and a connection between R' and folly and badness (for the ignorant is the foolish and bad man in a given activity).

It remains to show a connection between R and righteousness and between R' and unrighteousness. This connection follows from my defense of premises 2a and 2b above. It is uncontroversial (hence I can safely infer) that the righteous and only the righteous man in his actions as such will attempt to have more profit in human life than the unrighteous man but not more than a righteous man, just as it is uncontroversial and can be safely inferred that the unrighteous and only the unrighteous man in his actions as such will have pleonexia with respect to profit in human life.

From premises 4 and 6 it obviously follows that:

7. The righteous man is wise and good (in his actions as such), whereas the unrighteous man is foolish and bad (in his actions as such, 350c10–11).

From premise 7 it obviously follows that:

8. Righteousness is excellence and wisdom, whereas unrighteousness is defect and foolishness (350d4–5).

8.2 Argument that the Righteous Are Happy

Lemma in hand, I now show that the righteous are happy and the unrighteous miserable. The first ten premises (numbered 9 through 18 below) are relatively unproblematic.

9. (Definition) Let P be a person, A an action done in background circumstances C, and x anything. Then A is the *function* of x just in case P can do A (in C) by means of x and either there is nothing else by means of which P can do A

(in C) or nothing else by means of which P can do A (in C) as well as by means of x (352e2–3).[21]

10. There is an excellence and a defect associated with anything that has a function (353b2–3).

11. Whatever has a function does its function well by means of the associated excellence, and does its function poorly by means of the associated defect (353c6–7).

12. Human beings can do actions such as taking care of, ruling over, and deliberating about things by means of their (human) souls, and either there is nothing else by means of which they can do such actions, or nothing else by means of which they can do such actions as well (353d3–8).

13. Human beings live as such by means of their (human) souls, and either there is nothing else by means of which they can so live, or nothing else by means of which they can so live as well (353d9–10).

It obviously follows from premises 9 and either 12 or 13 that:

14. The human soul has a function (353d3).

It obviously follows from premises 9 and 13 that:

15. The human soul's function is human living as such (353d9).

It obviously follows from premises 10 and 14 that:

16. There is an excellence and a defect associated with the human soul (353d11).

It obviously follows from premises 11 and 14 that:

17. The human soul does its function well by means of the associated excellence, and does its function poorly by means of the associated defect (353e1–2).

The lemma proved that righteousness is excellence and wisdom, and unrighteousness defect and foolishness. From the lemma it follows that:

18. Righteousness is the excellence and unrighteousness the defect of the human soul (353e7–8).

The inference to premise 18 is less than obvious.[22] According to the lemma, righteousness is excellence. It follows that the activity that the righteous human being attempts as such is done well. And, as shown in the discussion of premise 2, the righteous human being attempts (in her

actions as such) to profit in human life as a whole. Therefore righteousness is excellence at human living as such. Hence, as an intermediate step,
righteousness *is* that by means of which human living as such is done well.
Notice now a consequence of premises 15 and 17: that by means of which
the human soul does well its function—namely, human living as such—
is the excellence of the human soul as such. From the intermediate step
and the consequence of 15 and 17, it follows that righteousness is the
excellence of the human soul as such. Similar remarks show that unrighteousness is the defect of the human soul as such.

Rick Creath, as I have understood him in conversation, has raised what
I call the aesthete's objection: as French language can distinguish, with
respect to gustatory pleasures, the *gourmand* from the *gourmet*, so with respect
to pleasures in general let me distinguish crude maximizers from refined
optimizers, that is, aesthetes. Socrates' argument refutes only the maximizer, not the optimizer. So Socrates' argument is particularly limited in
scope. After all, the error in life that the crude maximizer makes is not
nearly so interesting as the possible error made by the refined but amoral
optimizer.

A distinction between species of aesthetic pleasures provides a reply to
this objection. But a prior precision must be made, between those who
practice a skill (or perform a skill-like activity) for the sake of something
else and those who practice or perform it for its own sake (see chapter 10
for elaboration). The aesthete in an activity will be none other than the
expert (or the one who performs with excellence) who does it for its own
sake, that is, the expert "in the precise sense" (a full interpretation of the
Socratic position in *Republic* I must account for the precision at both 341c
and 346c; I cannot provide that here). For example, the aesthete with respect to the pleasures of weaving will be none other than the expert weaver
who weaves not for money nor out of the need for some fabric, but who
weaves for its own sake. Thus aesthetic pleasures are specified in one-one
correspondence to skills or skill-like excellences. And the lemma entails that
just as the aesthete about weaving pleasures will be none other than the one
who is excellent at weaving, that is, the weaver in the precise sense, so too
the aesthete about true human pleasure will be none other than the one who
is excellent at human living as such, that is, the righteous person.

Now to reply: the aesthetes of the objection either are or are not aesthetes about true human pleasure. If they are, they have been Socratically
demonstrated to be righteous. If they are not, then the fact that they optimize some other species of pleasure does not save them from Socrates'
argument, for they must crudely maximize in their seeking of *human* pleasure, even while able to optimize, say, *weaving* pleasures. For example,

weaving aesthetes, by virtue of their expertise, will not overdo the activities that constitute their weaving pleasures, but they either would or would not be unrighteous to sustain their enjoyment of optimal weaving pleasures. If they would be unrighteous, they have been Socratically demonstrated to be crude maximizers of human pleasure, despite their optimization of weaving pleasure. As such maximizers, the argument applies precisely to them. Hence Socrates' argument accounts for *gourmets* as well as *gourmands* and is not particularly limited.

From premises 15, 17, and 18 it obviously follows that:

19. The righteous human soul lives well (as a human soul); the unrighteous poorly (353e10–11).

It follows from premise 19 that:

20. The righteous human being lives well (as a human being); the unrighteous poorly (353e10–11).

Aristotle raises an objection to this inference.[23] "Perhaps the difference between possession and action, between having and using a function, is not negligible. For someone might have something without producing any good as a result" (*NE* I.8 1098b31–33). For example, someone might possess an excellent knife yet not cut, excellent musical skill yet not tune, or excellent medical skill yet not heal. For possession does not entail activity. Just so, Aristotle would object that someone might possess a righteous soul yet not live well.

A1. For possession of virtue [that is, a righteous soul] seems actually compatible with being asleep, or with lifelong inactivity, and, further, with the greatest sufferings and misfortunes; but a man who was living so no one would call happy, unless he were maintaining a thesis at all costs (*NE* I.5 1095b32–1096a2, trans. Ross).

There are two reasons why I might possess something with excellence in its function yet not use it. I might not attempt to or I might lack necessary conditions for its use. The first reason, not attempting, never applies to the case of excellent souls, for we all attempt to have profit from our lives.

Aristotle believes that the second reason applies, that lack of necessary conditions can prevent the one who possesses a righteous soul from the activities of living well.

A2. [Living well] needs the external goods . . . for it is impossible, or not easy, to do noble acts without the proper equipment. In many actions we use friends and riches and political power as instruments; and there are some things the lack of which takes the lustre from happiness—good birth, goodly children, beauty; for the man who is very ugly in appearance or ill-born or solitary and childless is not very likely to be happy, and perhaps a man would be still less likely if he had thoroughly bad children or friends or had lost good children or friends by death. As we said, then, happiness seems to need this sort of prosperity in addition [to possession of a righteous soul] (*NE* I.8 1099a31–b7, trans. Ross).

Notice that the objection is not to the equivalence of living righteously and living well as a human being. Such an objection would belong elsewhere, either to the truth of premises 15, 17, or 18, or to the validity of the inference to 19. Therefore, to meet Aristotle's objection, it will be enough to show that whoever *possesses* a righteous soul is in the necessary condition *actually to live* righteously. Aristotle's claim that possession of an excellence is compatible with its inactivity may be true for, say, excellence as a lover, a mother, or a political leader. But such excellences are not righteousness. The necessary background circumstances for righteous activity are found in times of poverty as well as prosperity, in times of torment as well as comfort (as Socrates points out at *La.* 191d and *Meno* 72a). For it is sufficient for righteous activity that a human being be able to care, rule, deliberate, and so forth regarding something. The object of the care and so forth may be friends, riches, political power, good birth, children, or external beauty, but it may as well be one's own soul in the absence of such external objects. So the external objects referred to in passage A2 do not show that possession of a righteous soul is compatible with inactivity of that soul.

Nonetheless Aristotle is right that there are certain circumstances under which one may possess an inactive soul, namely, those circumstances under which one is unable to take care and so forth. Such circumstances, suggested by passage A1—sleep and the greatest sufferings—are found in cases of unconsciousness and certain cases of altered consciousness produced by such things as extremes of mental illness, drug dosage, or overpowering sensations of emotion, pleasure, or pain. Now such circumstances will be of either occasional or terminal duration. But in neither case do they prevent one's life from actually being lived righteously. They do, of course, shorten the time of one's soul's activities. But length of activity is irrelevant to righteousness of activity; no one would call a shorter life a less righteous life.[24] So Aristotle's objection fails.

One more premise:

21. Whoever lives well is happy; whoever lives poorly is miserable (354a1–2).

It obviously follows from premises 20 and 21 that:

22. The righteous are happy; the unrighteous miserable (354a4).

8.3 Corollaries of the Argument

The corollary that Socrates draws from this argument requires one more uncontroversial premise:

23. It is unprofitable to be miserable but profitable to be happy (354a6).

From the argument's conclusion (that the righteous are happy and the unrighteous miserable) and premise 23, the corollary follows:

24. Unrighteousness is never more profitable than righteousness (354a8–9).

There are other corollaries of interest that are not drawn in the *Republic*. For instance, it follows that nothing bad can happen to a good man (*Ap.* 41d1). Another corollary, needed to make compelling the reconciliation of Socrates the hedonist with Socrates the virtue supremacist, is that living virtuously and living pleasantly are one and the same for a human being. I draw this corollary in chapter 10.

NINE

Does Socrates Consistently Hold
the Sufficiency Thesis?

In Chapter 8 Socrates was shown to give a compelling argument that the possession of virtue is sufficient for happiness. But there are other passages where Socrates appears committed to its insufficiency.[1] These apparently conflicting texts throw into darkness the question over which I have spun such a coil of argument. They raise the worry that there is no coherent ethical theory to be found in the Socratic dialogues, which in turn would resurrect the controversy whether these dialogues are even meant to convey an underlying philosophical position. Does Socrates affirm or deny the one-sentence answer that the possession of virtue is sufficient for happiness? Do the texts contradict each other? In this chapter I try to resolve this problem, in order to show that Socrates can consistently as well as compellingly hold that virtue is the good, that it is sufficient for human happiness. Because of their superior presentation of the problem, I focus on the work of Brickhouse and Smith.

9.1 Passages Supporting the Insufficiency Reading

At *Crito* 47e3–5, Socrates and Crito agree that life is not worth living with a body corrupted by disease. On the basis of this passage, one might attribute the following reasoning to Socrates (see Brickhouse and Smith 1994: 115):

1. Bodily disease can make life not worth living.
2. To live a life not worth living cannot be happiness.
3. Thus, the happiness of even a virtuous person can be destroyed.

But conclusion 3 does not follow. If the virtuous person does not choose to live with a corrupted body (and if death is no harm to her happiness— but there is no question that Socrates believes death is harmless to a virtuous person), then premise 1 is no reason to fear for her happiness. To be valid, the argument to conclusion 3 requires some additional premise, such as:

4. The virtuous person will choose to stay alive when the choice is a future with a body corrupted by disease.

But certainly Socrates does not accept premise 4. For one point of the *Crito* passage is that, just as it is rational to prefer death to life with a body corrupted by disease, so much the more ought we prefer death to life with a corrupted soul. The "just as" clause proves Socrates does not accept premise 4.

But, one might ask, what about the case where the virtuous person is forced to live with a wretched body, say, by tyrannical violence or religious prohibitions on suicide? The religious prohibition appears to be a fact for Socrates, according to *Phaedo* 61c–62c (though *Laws* IX 873c may offer an escape clause for those with bodies corrupted by disease); and the possibility of tyrannical violence is emphasized to Socrates (not a bit to his surprise) by Polus at *Gorgias* 473c1–5. If I add to premises 1 and 2:

5. The virtuous person might be forced (for example by violence or dogma) to live with a body corrupted by disease,

then conclusion 3 appears to follow.[2]

But the evidence of the *Crito* does not compel the attribution of this argument to Socrates. For premise 1 is ambiguous. It says a certain sort of life is not *biôton*, "to be lived," which might mean (*a*) it is not worth choosing or (*b*) it is wretched whether voluntarily or involuntarily lived. The context of this passage supports sense *a*. The point of the line of inquiry of which this passage is a part is that the rational one seeks not to maximize the length but to optimize the quality of one's life ("not to live . . . but to live well," *Cri.* 48b5). The point, therefore, concerns what one ought rationally to choose, not what is absolutely wretched as a fate whether voluntarily or involuntarily undergone.

Notice that if premise 1 is read in sense *a*, the conclusion 3 does not follow. Socrates might believe that if a person, even one with a virtuous soul, voluntarily chooses to live with a body corrupted by disease, then that choice would be an evil and bring the person harm. But it does not follow that if such a person involuntarily suffered such a fate, that fate would be an evil bringing the person harm. Likewise in the *Apology*, Socrates makes it clear that his voluntary choice of prison, fines, exile, and ceasing to philosophize would be evils that would harm him (37b–38a). It does not follow, however, that Socrates' involuntary suffering any of these fates would be evils that harm him. For, if the *Phaedo* is to be trusted, Socrates would have regarded his own voluntary choice of suicide as an evil that would have harmed him; even so, he surely would not have changed his assessment that his involuntary suffering of death was harmless.

Consider next the similar passage at *Gorgias* 512a2–5: "If someone [has a body corrupted by disease], he is wretched because he did not die, and [someone who preserves his life] does him no good." This passage appears to support the same argument as the *Crito* passage, and my comments are the same, except my claim that depended on an ambiguity I found in *biôton*. There is no such ambiguity here. Nor is it possible to dismiss this passage by noticing that Socrates does not assert this evaluation in his own person but asserts that another, a pilot, might reckon thus. For a pilot certainly would not reckon as Socrates predicts here, unless under the stimulus of a Socratic cross-examination. But the point of the examination is the same as that established in the *Crito*, which is not to contend that a certain level of bodily disease is an absolute evil, but rather that it is a mistake to focus one's attention on living as long as possible (*Grg.* 511b), that one ought to leave the length of one's life to God and focus one's attention on the best way to live the life that one is to have (*Grg.* 512e). A comprehensive reading of this passage, such as follows, attends to these factors:

> Socrates gets Callicles to agree in the end that health is the good of the body and virtue is the good of the soul, and that the latter is an immeasurably greater good than the former, because the soul is "so much more precious than the body" (512a5–6; see 477b5–e6, *Cri.* 47e6–48a3). If the good of the body should come into conflict with the good of the soul, or should in some way contribute to the evil of the soul (e.g., if one's good health enabled one to pursue more actively a life of evil and injustice—see *Euthyd.* 281b4–e1), then health would become, all things considered, an evil [and

likewise disease might become a good]. The point here is not simply that health is less important than virtue; rather, it is that health is not *always* a good [nor disease always an evil, Brickhouse and Smith 1994: 112; comments in square brackets mine].

My conclusion about the *Crito* and *Gorgias* passages is as follows. The claim that these passages explicitly entail the insufficiency of virtue's possession for happiness is false.[3] These passages entail the insufficiency only if one interprets the *Crito* by choosing a sense of *biôton* not compelled by the context, and only if one interprets the prediction about what a pilot would say in a way that can sensibly be rejected. So these passages give little reason to give up the truism that Socrates maintains the sufficiency of virtue's possession for human happiness.

There are other passages. At *Apology* 38a, Socrates says, "The unexamined life is not worth living for a human being." One might conclude that this passage "shows he requires more than a good soul to make his life worth living" (Brickhouse and Smith 1994: 117). But this conclusion does not follow. Death, of course, will not be a harm for Socrates. And banishment to an uninhabited island will not keep him from self-examination. I made the same point in section 8.2 in resisting Aristotle's criticism of the philosophical thesis that the mere possession of virtue is sufficient for happiness. So long as one is able to take care, even if only of one's own soul, one will be able to engage in virtuous activity. To terminate that ability is, with respect to harm, equivalent to death: it will shorten but not ruin or harm one's active life.

In defense of their statement that there is an important Socratic distinction between possessing a virtuous soul and engaging in virtuous activity, Brickhouse and Smith cite *Gorgias* 507b5–c5. Let me distinguish three statements within this passage.

A. "The temperate one [that is, the one possessing a virtuous soul] is [disposed to] pursue or flee from the affairs, and men, and pleasures, and pains which he ought to flee and pursue."

B. "The good person [that is, the one possessing a virtuous soul] acts well and nobly in what he does."

C. "The one who does well is blessed and happy."

They assert that this passage shows that "the correct 'management and rule' that constitutes the proper functioning of the soul concerns the appropriate 'avoidance and pursuit of things and people'" (Brickhouse and Smith 1994: 114). I agree, so long as they mean by "things" even pleasures and pains, as mentioned in statement *A*, which are of course internal to the soul, and so long as they allow that one need not be faced with *all*, but merely *any* of these things, to display genuine temperance or virtue. But they conclude: "Thus, the good soul is concerned with good action and not merely the maintenance of its own good condition." It would be more accurate to say that the good soul is concerned with good action, *including* the action of maintaining its own good condition. Of course it would be evil and harm me voluntarily to concern myself *only* with the improvement of my soul to the exclusion of all other's interests (though I doubt that it could be possible to conjoin self-improvement with neglect of others). But if my fate were to suffer a banishment in solitude, Socrates would evidently hold, according to statement *B*, that I would still do well in what I did, presumably even if that doing was limited to soul maintenance, and thus, by statement *C*, be happy. Notice that even in solitude there are pleasures and pains to avoid and pursue, and thus genuine temperance can be activated. I agree that acting well, not the mere possession of a good soul, brings happiness. But, as I have argued, the possession of virtue entails its activity. Thus, with respect to achieving happiness, there is not after all any significant distinction between the possession and the activity of virtue, such as in the claim of Brickhouse and Smith that souls possessing virtue might not but souls engaging in virtuous activity must be happy.

9.2 Passages Supporting the Sufficiency Reading

Let me now turn to the passages that appear to commit Socrates to the sufficiency thesis. In addition to the argument of *Republic* I—in particular 353e10–11: "The just soul and the just person will live well"—there is also *Gorgias* 470e, where Socrates asserts: "The good and noble man and woman is happy."[4] Brickhouse and Smith interpret these passages as follows:

> Socrates may be referring to goodness and justice in persons *as they are under ordinary circumstances*, that is, suffering no substantially impaired capacity for the sort of agency one could, *ceteris paribus*, expect from the good man or woman. If Polus or Thrasymachus had interrupted in either passage with the question, "Do you mean, Socrates, that a virtuous person would live well even if he was systematically prevented from doing his soul's virtuous bidding, due to disease, infirmity, or an injustice done to him?" we should expect a more carefully qualified presentation of Socrates' position. (1994: 119)[5]

For this interpretation to be tenable, there must be, in the context of these passages, no mention of circumstances that prevent the activities of a good soul. But impediments to virtuous activity due to physical or social incapacities are an explicit part of the context of both passages. In the *Gorgias*, Callicles asserts that either suffering wrong at the hands of another or the vocation of philosophy will systematically prevent one from doing one's soul's bidding, in the first case because of the injustice done one, in the second case because of the infirmities produced by over-attention to philosophy.

The Calliclean speeches I quote all occur later in the dialogue than Socrates' assertion at 470e. Yet both Socrates and Callicles recognize their discussion as a continuation of the same discussion Socrates had with Polus (487a–b; all these passages trans. by Woodhead; italics mine).

> To suffer wrong is not even fit for a man but only for a slave, for whom it is better to be dead than alive, since when wronged and outraged *he is unable to help* himself or any other for whom he cares. (483a–b)

> Philosophy . . . , if you continue in it longer than you should, is the ruin of any man. For if a man is exceptionally gifted and yet pursues philosophy far on in life, he must prove entirely unacquainted with all the accomplishments requisite for a gentleman and a man of distinction . . . and so *when they enter upon any activity public or private they appear ridiculous.* (484c–d)

> [A man who practices philosophy], even if exceptionally gifted, is doomed to prove less than a man, shunning the city center and market place, in which the poet said that men win distinction. (485d)

> Do you not consider it a disgrace to be in the condition I think you are in . . . ? For now if anyone should seize you or any others like you and drag you off to prison, claiming you are guilty when you are not, you realize that *you would not know what to do*, but you would reel to and fro and gape openmouthed, without a word to say, and when you came before the court, even with an utterly mean and rascally accuser, you would be put to death, if he chose to demand the death penalty. And yet what wisdom is there in this, Socrates, in "an art which finds a man well-gifted and leaves him worse"—*able neither to help himself nor to save from the extremes of danger either himself or anybody else*, but fated to be robbed by his enemies of all his property and to live literally like one disfranchised in his own city? (486a–c)

Callicles' assertion that the lifelong practice of philosophy increases one's vulnerability to prison, fines, death, and the like is indisputable in the case of Socrates' own life. If those results can make a life wretched, as

Brickhouse and Smith assert, then Socrates has sufficient reason not to practice philosophy—but no one would attribute such a view to Socrates.

Likewise in *Republic* I, Thrasymachus asserts that the mere possession of virtue in one's soul will systematically prevent one from doing one's soul's bidding, because of social incapacities it must inevitably produce. Thrasymachus asserts:

> The just man (that is, the one who possesses a virtuous soul) always comes out at a disadvantage in his relation with the unjust. To begin with, in their business dealings in any joint undertaking of the two you will never find that the just man has the advantage over the unjust at the dissolution of the partnership but that he always has the worst of it. Then again, in their relations with the state, if there are direct taxes or contributions to be paid, the just man contributes more from an equal estate and the other less, and when there is a distribution the one gains much and the other nothing. And so when each holds office, apart from any other loss the just man must count on his own affairs' falling into disorder through neglect, while because of his justice he makes no profit from the state, and thereto he will displease his friends and his acquaintances by his unwillingness to serve them unjustly. (343d–e, trans. Shorey)

Thrasymachus recognizes that his claim that the ruthless tyrant is most powerful is of a piece with his claim that possessing a virtuous soul systematically incapacitates one:

> The easiest way of all to understand this matter will be to turn to the most consummate form of injustice [that is, the tyrant]. (344a, trans. Shorey)

It would in any case be incredible to suggest that a ceteris paribus qualification be attached to Socrates' statements at *Apology* 30c8–d1: "Neither Meletus nor Anytus could harm me—that is not possible—for I do not think it is permitted for a better person to be harmed by a worse," and *Apology* 41d1–2: "No evil comes to a good person either in life or in death." Let us imagine here that Meletus or a juror pose the same question to Socrates as Brickhouse and Smith (1994: 119) hypothetically put in the mouths of Polus and Thrasymachus:

> If [Meletus or a juror] had interrupted in this passage with the question, "Do you mean, Socrates, that a virtuous person would be unharmed even if he was systematically prevented from doing his soul's virtuous bidding, due to disease, infirmity, or an injustice done to him, such as exile, fines, prison or death?"

We can be certain that Socrates would reply: "That is exactly what I am saying: indeed, even if the injustice were death one hundred times over" (see *Ap.* 30c).

Regarding these passages from the *Apology*, Brickhouse and Smith (1994: 121) claim that "unless we are to convict him of self-contradiction within the briefest of passages, he cannot mean that moral goodness, by itself, is always sufficient for happiness." There are two such apparently contradictory passages. At *Apology* 41d4–5, Socrates argues: "To die and be released from my *pragmata* is better for me." *Pragmata* might mean Socrates' life's work, his mission and all it has brought him, or the narrower translation, "troubles" used by Brickhouse and Smith. In either case, the passage neither says nor implies that Socrates' life is no longer worth living nor that he has been harmed. One option can be better than another without it being the case that the second option is so bad that it is not worth living and without it being the case that either option is harmful. The same point applies to *Apology* 42a2–5, where Socrates suggests it is possible that some members of the jury go to a better fate than his: even had Socrates said it was a certainty that some jurors had a better lot than he, it would not follow that his life would not be worth living or that he had been harmed.[6]

9.3 Conclusion

There are two prima facie contradictory sets of passages. One set appears to establish Socrates' belief in the insufficiency, the other in the sufficiency of the possession of virtue for happiness. Our choices are either to give up an attempt at a coherent Socratic ethical theory or reinterpret one or other set of passages in harmony with the other.[7] Charity should lead us to look for coherence, but it should not, or so I have argued (see n. 1), lead us to prefer an insufficiency to a sufficiency thesis. And while a coherent and plausible exegesis can be given that attributes the sufficiency thesis to Socrates, an attempt to attribute the insufficiency thesis to Socrates is implausible. Thus I am now able to establish the thesis of this book, which is the work of chapter 10.

TEN

How Socrates Can Make Both Pleasure
and Virtue the Chief Good

Most scholars think that when Socrates argued in the first book of the *Republic* that the possession of virtue is sufficient for happiness, his argument failed (see chapter 8, n. 2). But, the alleged weakness of that argument notwithstanding, there is almost no dispute that Socrates accepted its conclusion, that the possession of virtue is sufficient for happiness.[1] Nor is there controversy over whether, according to Socrates, virtue is instrumentally good. There is little controversy whether virtue for Socrates is intrinsically good.[2] There has been deep controversy stemming from the fact that the Socrates featured in the early dialogues claims all of the following:

1. Pleasure is not the good for human beings (in the *Gorgias*).
2. Pleasure is the good for human beings (in the *Protagoras*).
3. Virtue is the good for human beings (in the *Apology* and *Crito*).

I have suggested (in chapters 3–5) a way to reconcile statements 1 and 2. After two theories of pleasure are distinguished, it is possible to show how Socrates argues against one in the *Gorgias* in a manner consistent with his acceptance of the theory he defends in the *Protagoras*. My task in this chapter is to show, by drawing together threads from chapters 6 to 9, how Socrates can reconcile statements 2 and 3. My strategy is to show how Socrates can identify pleasant activity, according to his theory of pleasure, with virtuous activity.

Many interpreters read the *Protagoras* as a dialogue where Plato is *either* merely trying out ideas without concern for their unity with other claims defended in other dialogues *or* merely using the hedonist assumption to gain a logical advantage without committing himself to the doctrine.[3] Such interpreters will be troubled by the significance I give to the hedonism of the *Protagoras* by making it a starting point of my work. This trouble comes from some such line of reasoning as follows. In the *Protagoras*, Socrates defends the claim that pleasure is the only good. But in the *Apology* and *Crito*, Socrates unquestionably believes that virtue is a good above all others. Socrates cannot have it both ways. Either virtue or pleasure may be the final good—but not both. Since the supremacy of virtue is unquestionable for Socrates, it would seem that hedonism is an impossible doctrine for Socrates to hold. But such a line of reasoning is flawed. For the assumption that not both pleasure and virtue can be the chief good is false as a claim about a Socratic account of pleasure.

10.1 An Aristotelian Account of Pleasure as Modal

Aristotle believes that a view of pleasure as modal is superior to theories that see the essence of pleasure in sensation:

> There is no great value in defining pleasure as a phenomenal event [*aisthêtên genesin*]: better to say it is an activity in accordance with the nature of one's condition [*energeian tês kata phusin hexeôs*], unimpeded [*anempodiston*, instead of phenomenal]. (*NE* VII.12 1153a13–15)

10.2 Socrates Held a Modal Account of Pleasure

As demonstrated in chapter 6, the *Apology* gives grounds for ascribing a modal notion of pleasure to Socrates. There Socrates argues that dreamless sleep—a sensationless activity—is a surpassing pleasure (40d6). If Socrates held a sensate account of pleasure, such a claim would be laughably false (as indeed it has seemed to sensatist interpreters). But, with a modal account of pleasure, a plausible defense can be given of this Socratic argument.

10.3 A Modal Account of Pleasure Allows
Socrates to Identify Pleasant Activity
with One Kind of Skillful Activity

Following Aristotle, I can say that a modal pleasure is an unimpeded activity in accordance with the nature of one's condition. If it is the nature of one's condition to be skillful (as, for example, in the case of a carpenter or weaver), then the activity in accordance with that nature will be the exercise of that skill (working with wood or weaving). Two cases need to be distinguished. Sometimes we do a skillful activity for its own sake; sometimes for the sake of something else.[4] In the second case weaving is done in subordination to a superordinate goal, perhaps money or repair. In this case there is no reason to suppose the action displays the symptoms of or is a modal pleasure. Indeed, strictly speaking, the person who engages in this activity, however skillfully, only for subordinate reasons, is more properly called by the name of the superordinate skill: moneymaker or home economist.[5] But in the first case, the weaving would be done as a leisure activity freely chosen. One might weave without needing the woven product; one might weave even in neglect of pressing needs. In such cases the activity of weaving is not toil for some superordinate necessity but is an expression of one's nature as a weaver. Pleasant activity for a weaver in this sense is nothing but the skillful activity of weaving. Weaving is an illustration; in general, this identity holds true for any insubordinate skillful activity.

10.4 A Modal Account of Pleasure Allows
Socrates to Identify Pleasant Activity
with Virtuous Activity

There is no question that for Socrates virtue is a matter of skill, not will (*Euthyd.* 278e–282e, *Meno* 77b–78b). And, while it is conceivable that one may perform a virtuous action for the sake of something else, such as prestige or money, a virtuous person, strictly speaking, chooses virtue in subordination to nothing else (*Ap.* 28b5–9, *Cri.* 48b–d). A virtuous person will accordingly freely choose to do virtuous activities. Because such activities express one's nature without impediment, they display the symptoms of and are modal pleasures. Lest such a view seem too otherworldly to attribute to Socrates, notice that even this-worldly Aristotle holds that virtuous activity is necessarily pleasant to the virtuous person (*NE* I.8 1099a7–21).

10.5 Socratic Argument Entails that, for a Human Being, Living Well, Living Pleasantly, and Living Virtuously Are One and the Same

Socrates might hold that, just as true pleasure *for a weaver* is weaving, so true pleasure *for a virtuous person* is virtuous activity. But the argument of *Republic* I (349b–354a, defended in chapter 8) enables Socrates to draw an even stronger conclusion: true pleasure *for any human being* is virtuous activity.[6] Just as the distinctive excellence of a weaver is weaving, Socrates argues that the distinctive excellence of a human being is virtue (*Rep.* I 353e7–8). Socrates explicitly—however paradoxically—concludes that the virtuous person will necessarily live well, blessedly, and happily. Even if one supposes that the *Protagoras*'s defense of hedonism had never been written (as some interpreters must wish, for all the trouble it has given them), it surely would not be out of character for Socrates to ask a few more questions after the conclusion of book I of the *Republic*:

> Do you think that one would be living well, blessedly, or happily, who spent life in pain and misery? [As *Prt.* 351b.]
> Impossible.
> Then if one lived happily and blessedly, could life be deficient in pleasure?
> No way, Socrates.
> So the virtuous live pleasantly, . . . and never can vice be more pleasant than virtue [for a human being].

These questions are not found in the *Republic* because the issue between Socrates and Thrasymachus concerns profit, not pleasure, in human life. But, as I maintain, such a sequence would not be out of character for Socrates.

10.6 Why Does Socrates Think Virtue Is Necessary for Happiness?— A Problem Solved

There is little doubt that Socrates believed not only that virtue was sufficient for happiness, but also that it was necessary.[7] But imagine a demon that told Socrates—the Socrates who is ignorant of virtue and therefore not virtuous—not merely what he should not do but also indicated magically what was the virtuous action for him at each point in his life. Socrates, by following these reliable ordinations, would appear to be blessed with as happy a life as anyone genuinely possessing the skill of virtue. Thus whoever, thanks to good luck, possessed such a demon would have no need of the skill of virtue. Given such a possibility, Socrates would be wrong to insist that virtue is necessary for happiness.

One solution to this problem—an uncharitable one—is to claim that Socrates was wrong; he neglected this possibility. This solution is plausible to the degree that my demonic thought experiment is far removed from Socrates' experience. But my thought experiment is at little or no distance from Socrates' experience. The demon of Socrates' actual experience kept him from wrongdoing.[8] There are two possibilities. It may be that one only avoids wrongdoing by doing what is best. In this case, the demon I have imagined is identical to the one of Socrates' experience. Or it may be that one can avoid wrongdoing yet fail to act virtuously. In this case the demon I have imagined is a superior version of the one in Socrates' experience: in addition to warning off from wrongdoing, it magically dictates the virtuous action to be performed. Such a possibility, while imaginary, is only a little removed from Socrates' experience. Thus this uncharitable solution is implausible.

A better solution is at hand on my hypothesis that Socrates held a modal account of pleasure and identified virtuous activity with pleasant activity. To see why, consider the case of a chess demon. By means of such a demon, let us suppose, one could play chess as well as any expert in chess. For chess players the (insubordinate) activity of playing chess is pleasure. Now it seems to me that, despite the comparable external victories shared by the true expert and the one guided by a super demon, the true expert will have incomparably deeper satisfaction in life. This has to do, I believe, with the fact that the pleasure of chess requires self-directed activity. The true expert is a master while the guided one remains forever an ignorant slave, as it were. I believe it is the lack of self-direction that spoils the fun for the guided chess player, despite impressive results. As a prizewinner or moneymaker such a one might take pleasure, but as a chess player one's pleasure would be defective. And my beliefs are Socratic: Socrates connects happiness with self-direction at *Lysis* 207e; he connects knowledge with self-direction at *Lysis* 210a–c. My point is that only the true expert, not the demonically guided nonexpert, can have unspoiled pleasure in the insubordinate exercise of a skill. This point is general, and includes, for Socrates, the case of the true human expert, that is, the virtuous person. Without the knowledge that is virtue, even if one had a super demon for guidance, one would lack the unspoiled pleasure of virtuous activity in which one's happiness as a human being consists.

The following lesson, in sum, may be learned from the case of the super demon. A satisfactory account of Socratic ethics must explain why the blessed life requires the performance of virtuous actions *with knowledge*. By ascribing a modal hedonism to Socrates, and identifying virtuous and pleasant activity, such an explanation can be given.

10.7 Conclusion

The hypothesis that Socrates held a modal, not sensate, account of pleasure is supported by the "death is one of two things" argument of the *Apology* and by the explanation such an account can make of Socrates' doctrine that virtue, not merely a helpful demon, is necessary for happiness. Moreover, on this hypothesis Socrates' identification of pleasant activity with skillful activity, and in the case of human beings, pleasant activity with virtuous activity, can be explained. Thus Socrates can make both pleasure and virtue the chief good for human beings, relieving the tension between the *Protagoras* and the *Apology* and *Crito*, between Socrates the inspiration and model for Epicureanism and for Stoicism, between Socrates the hedonist and Socrates the virtue supremacist.

Notes

Chapter 1

1. Scholars tend to agree that the following dialogues of Plato contain a portrait of Socrates rather than act as a mouthpiece for Plato's later views: *Ap.*, *Cri.*, *Chrm.*, *La.*, *Lys.*, *Euthphr.*, *Hp. Mi.*, *Ion*, *Prt.*, and *Rep.* I. Dialogues often seen as divided between the portrait/mouthpiece distinction are the *Grg.*, *Meno*, *Euthyd.*, *Hp. Ma.*, and *Pho.* See for example Dodds (1959: 18–30), Brickhouse and Smith (1989: 1–13), Penner (1992: 121–130), and Irwin (1995: 4–16). But it is possible to be skeptical about such a division, as are Nails (1995: 53–68), Kahn (1996: 44–46) and Cooper (1997: xii–xvii). It is uncontroversial to make *Ap.* the starting point of an investigation of Socratic ethics. I argue in this book that *Grg.* and *Prt.* are consistent with each other and with *Ap.*, using an argument from *Rep.* I to provide a key step in my argument. So a consequence of this book is that the doctrinal content of the *Prt.*, *Grg.*, and *Rep.* I will no longer be a reason to separate these dialogues into different periods from each other or from the *Ap.* But this book's concern is the philosophical ideas in these dialogues, rather than the historical issues of to whom to attribute the ideas or at which developmental stage Plato wrote which dialogue.

2. For example, Grote 1865 and Guthrie 1975.

3. For example, Brandis 1835, Zeller 1888, Crombie 1962, and Irwin 1995.

4. Those who argue that Socrates is a hedonist include Grote 1865, Hackforth 1928, Dodds 1959, Irwin 1977 (see also Irwin 1995: 81–92, who qualifies his argu-

ment), and Gosling and Taylor 1982. Those who argue he is not, include Taylor 1929, Moreau 1939, Sullivan 1961, Vlastos 1969, Zeyl 1989, and Kahn 1996.

5. Vlastos (1991: 6) likewise holds that the biggest of the fundamental questions about Socrates "is whether or not the moral philosophy in Plato's dialogues is broadly utilitarian."

6. Gómez-Lobo (1994: 5) and Vlastos (1991: 214, n. 59) also place Socrates outside both Kantianism and Utilitarianism, though neither identifies human pleasure with virtuous activity.

7. Gosling and Taylor 1982 likewise distinguish different species of hedonism in order to reconcile the two dialogues.

8. This is, for instance, the interpretation of Dent 1984.

9. Roochnik (1985: 214) is a recent example of a sensatist interpreter.

10. This distinction is in Aristotle, *NE* I.1 1094a2–5; in Plato, *Rep.* II 357b–d, and is suggested by the Socratic distinction at *Grg.* 467c–468a and aporia at *Lys.* 218d–222e.

11. This precision is observed by Socrates at *Rep.* I 341c–d and 345c–d.

Chapter 2

1. See Griswold 1985. For other philosophical purposes served by the dialogue form, see Cooper 1997: xviii–xxiii.

2. See for example the readings given by Woodruff 1982, Haden 1983, Nussbaum 1986, and Stokes 1986.

3. See Kahn 1983, reiterated in his 1996: 137.

4. Thus my concern is distinct from concern with Socratic cross-examination (*elenchus*) within the dialogue: mine is with Plato's purposes in writing dialogues; the other concern is with Socrates' purposes in speaking in dialogues. *Oxford Studies in Ancient Philosophy* has published notable discussion of Socrates' purposes: see volumes 1, 3, and 4.

5. See Irwin (1995: 4–16) for a sensible discussion of this controversy.

6. See more recently Teloh (1981: 46): "For pedagogical reasons Plato ends the early dialogues with contrived fallacies and invented paradoxes the answers to which are found in those dialogues." Teloh's analysis is on pp. 46–64.

7. More recently there is Guthrie 1975: 130–131.

8. For discussion of the esoterist position and its relation to Neoplatonic readings, see Tigerstedt 1977: 63–90.

9. For a similar interpretation of the Stranger's behavior in *Soph.*, see Rudebusch 1991.

10. Irwin (1995: 7–8) sees this pedagogical reason for the dialogue form and uses it to explain why Plato wrote dialogues. As I point out in the following paragraph, this reason does not explain why someone might write aporetic rather than merely expository dialogues.

11. This picture of the dialogues is inspired by Penner's seminar work with graduate students, which unfortunately is largely unpublished. However, see his 1973a and 1973b.

Chapter 3

1. The conflicts are well stated by Gosling and Taylor 1982: 69–70.

2. Gosling and Taylor are followed by Berman (1991b: 126) and Irwin (1995: 89). Tarrant (1994: 117–118) makes a similar distinction between "what is ultimately pleasantest" and "what is pleasantest in the short term," though he does not accept the reconciliation of Gosling and Taylor.

3. "Verbals in . . . -tea . . . express necessity" (Smyth 1956 sec. 473; see also sec. 358.2). Hence *ou praktea* has the form "necessarily not-P."

4. I follow Irwin (1977: 106–107), Wiggins (1978–79), Nussbaum (1986: 113–116), and Brickhouse and Smith (1994: 97). I consider my cases to be mere elaboration on Nussbaum's bagel example. Richardson 1990 argues that the text does not force us to choose between comparability and commensurability. But he does not show how Socrates' argument can succeed if it assumes only comparability.

5. I draw the last two examples, novelty and fetish, from Stocker (1990: 226).

6. Taylor (1980: 506) does not recognize the importance of the commensurability thesis to Socrates' case against *akrasia*: "I doubt whether the [hypothesis of hedonism] is of any significance." His example of adultery (1990: 501), which he uses to establish that there is *akrasia*, is not like case 4. Thus it begs the question from Plato by assuming there is no single standard of measurement.

Irwin (1977: 107) believes that we might accept the commensurability thesis yet still allow for *akrasia* if we deny what he calls principle *P*: "When *A* chooses *x* over *y*, he chooses it because he values *x* more than *y*." Irwin claims that principle *P* "does not follow" from the commensurability thesis, but I see no way to deny principle *P* in cases like 4, and cases unlike 4 implicitly abandon the commensurability thesis. (Irwin 1995: 84, no longer makes this claim of invalidity.) The same sort of reply can be made to Santas (1979: ch. 7) and Gallop (1964: 127–128).

Stocker (1990: 225) claims that such cases as 3 can be cases of a simple more against less and *akrasia* nonetheless can be possible:

> There are various ways to argue that such a choice of the lesser over the better is possible. One is in terms of . . . "spiritual maladies" . . . e.g. timidity, lack of confidence, tiredness, depression, and accidie. People suffering from these conditions . . . naturally turn away from what is best, *as being too much or too good for them, or simply as not being for them.* . . . [They] do not seek moderation. They, rather, avoid what they think is best . . . because, as we might say, their desires or their spirits are too weak. [Italics mine.]

But, as the italicized phrase shows, such people are averse to what is best not simpliciter but qua inappropriate. Stocker anticipates and argues against the assumption that such people desire moderation. I make no such assumption. There are two cases to consider. (1) Some people, in addition to desiring more, are averse to what they believe they deserve. Given both desire and aversion, we cannot in this sort of case plausibly attribute a single standard of more or less (likewise with his cases of novelty and fetish, Stocker 1990: 226). (2) Some people, without any aversions, simply lack desire for more; they are indifferent to small or big pay raises. Such people are not *akratic*.

See for example Davidson 1970, Watson 1977, Mele 1987, Belgum 1990, and Penner 1990 for further discussion of the impossibility of *akrasia*.

7. Gosling and Taylor (1982: 57–58) are aware of this problem, but they present it as a problem for Socrates' argument, not as a problem for their own interpretation. Likewise Irwin (1995: 107).

8. My understanding of the refutation of Polus is indebted to graduate work with Penner in the late seventies. See Penner 1988 and 1991. I do not discuss *Grg*. 474–475; for a successful interpretation see Berman 1991a.

9. He argues that reality in itself must be completely indeterminate: "all is in flux." I follow Terry Penner's unpublished account (see Penner 1987: 317) of this overall theory, its power, and its relation to forms of verificationism, Kantianism, and empiricism. White (1979: 160) has noted that Protagoreanism was Plato's opponent from the time of the earliest dialogues. This lifelong opposition unites Plato's body of dialogues and underlies his theory of Forms.

10. I am taking Descartes to claim in the second *Meditation* that although *what* he doubts (for example his body's existence) is a matter for skeptical doubt, *that* he doubts his body's existence is not. Although *what* he desires (for example this glass of milk) is a matter for doubt, *that* he desires this glass of milk is not. And likewise with conceiving, feeling confident, affirming, denying, willing, rejecting, imagining, and perceiving.

11. Things that are at once possibly extrinsically desirable and possibly extrinsically undesirable are called by Socrates "the things which are neither good nor bad" (*oute agathon oute kakon*, 467e3; see also e6–7) or which are "in between" (*metaxu*, 467e2, 468b1), which "take part (*metechei*) sometimes in the good, sometimes the bad, and sometimes neither" (467e7–468a1). Things that are in fact extrinsically desirable (therefore in fact not extrinsically undesirable) he calls "beneficial" (*ôphelima*, 468c4). Things that are in fact intrinsically undesirable (therefore in fact not extrinsically desirable) he calls "harmful" (*blabera*, 468c4).

12. Socrates here calls intrinsic desirables and undesirables "good things" and "bad things" (*ta agatha* by parity with *ta kaka*, 467e5); both are "that for the sake of which we do things" (*ekeino hou heneka prattei*, 467d7–e1), either to seek the good or to avoid the bad.

13. In Aristotle's terminology, the intrinsically desirable is the "end" (*telos*, *NE* I.2 1094a18) or "good" (*tagathon kai to ariston*, 1094a22); the extrinsic desirables are "the [things leading] to the end" (*ta pros to telos*; see III.2 1111b27).

14. Socrates uses roughly the same terms to describe both that which is unconditionally desired and the intrinsically desirable: it is called "the good," "the thing pursued" (468b1) or "that for the sake of which we do things" (b7, b9). That which is conditionally desired he calls "that which is thought to be [for] the better [or best]" (b2, d3), "that which seems better" (e2) or for the best (d4; see also 466c2, d2–3, e2, e9–10, 467a3, a5, b3–4, b8). There is one minor difference: when he is using "what is desired" as opposed to what is conditionally desired, he tends to use plural relative pronouns (466c9–d1, e1, 467b2, b6, 468d5, d7, and e6, but note the singular use at 466b11–c1); when it is opposed to what is extrinsically desired, he uses singular relative pronouns (467c5–7, c10–d5, d7–e1, 468b3, c1).

15. For further discussion of its significance, see Penner 1988 and Rudebusch 1988.

Chapter 4

1. The etymology of the verb suggests the image of the appetite as a trireme, the one possessing the appetite having the role of a rower in relation to it.

2. I follow Parfit (1984: 493) and Brink (1989: 67) in these distinctions between theories of self-interest, rationality, and ethics.

3. Santas (1979: 254–286) has worked out most carefully this interpretation.

4. Recent commentators agree that the argument, seen as directed against prudential hedonism, fails: Irwin (1977: 120–121; 1979: 202; 1995: 107), Santas (1979: 268–270), and Gosling and Taylor (1982: 73–74).

5. That the argument from pleased cowards fails to refute prudential hedonism is seen by Irwin (1977: 121; 1979: 203–204) and Gosling and Taylor (1982: 74–75). Santas (1979: 280–284) defends this argument, but he seems not to recognize that the prudential hedonist need not be committed to the claim that all aspects of a good life are decisively more pleasant than a bad life, only that some are.

6. For such an interpretation, see Irwin (1977: 121, 1979: 205–206, 1995: 107–108) and Kahn (1983: 109).

7. For such an interpretation, see Irwin (1977: 121–122, 1979: 203–204) and Kahn (1983: 105–109).

8. As Kahn (1983: 104) claims without giving supporting evidence.

9. Kahn argues that "the selective hedonism of a successful politician or business-man is only superficially stronger than Callicles' unrestricted version, since if this selection is to be articulated as a rational theory it will require some principle of preference," which for a hedonist can only be their quantitative contributions to overall pleasure and pain (1983: 104–105). Kahn attempts to explain why the dialogue neglects a consideration of such a position on the grounds of Callicles' "hot blood," which prevents him from proposing "such cold calculations" (1983: 105, n. 51). Dramatically this is unpersuasive: where is Callicles portrayed as hot-blooded any more than as coldly calculating? In any case, Callicles does not neglect the quantitative importance of appetites at *Grg.* 491e9–492a2. And, to leave aside questions of dramatic interpretation, there remains a sense of failure about this dialogue if Plato is seen only to deal with a hot-blooded defense of the life-style of tyrants and orators; how does Plato hope to change the tyrannical and oratorical aspirations of those in his audience who are cold-blooded?

Benson (1990: 2) has commented that this failure to destroy in general the esteem of oratorical power may not be an unacceptable consequence for an interpretation of *Grg.*, for "Calliclean hedonism and its Socratic refutation are only part of a much larger argument" against common esteem of oratorical power.

I agree that *if* an indiscriminate, licentious, or sybaritic interpretation of Callicles can show how *Grg.* as a whole refutes in general the esteem of oratorical power, then such an interpretation will not be vulnerable to this particular criticism. But I am skeptical of the antecedent.

10. For this interpretation, see Gosling and Taylor (1982: 71–75).

11. Benson (1990: 2) has commented that this failure to destroy in general the esteem of oratorical power may not be an unacceptable consequence. See note 9.

12. Socrates gives examples of such processes: flute playing, lyre playing, and the like; choruses and dithyrambic poetry; singing to the lyre; tragic drama; and the rhetorical public address of demagogues, including political oratory (*Grg.* 501d–502d).

13. "To live as long as possible" is stated as a possible object of one's preparations (*Grg.* 511b8–9); presumably it could be the object of one's appetite in such a case.

14. Parfit (1984: 493), for example, draws this distinction. My "stimulation" is his "narrow" hedonism; my "satisfaction" is his "preference" hedonism. In section 6.3 I distinguish "sensate" from "modal" pleasure. These are different sets of distinctions. The sensate theorist could be a hedonist of stimulation or satisfaction; the modal theorist might but need not be a satisfaction hedonist.

15. Benson (1990: 4) comments that "in claiming that pleasure is the *satisfaction* of appetites, Callicles comes dangerously close [on my interpretation] to simply claiming that pleasure is the *release* from pain." Such a consequence would be disastrous for my interpretation. For on such an account, "stones and corpses would be supremely happy," as Callicles points out (492e) in explicitly rejecting Socrates' stable ideal of being released from pain for his own dynamic ideal of "the largest possible influx" (494b).

But Callicles' position, as I have interpreted it, is in no such danger. The expression "satisfaction of appetites" can mean either the state of being satisfied or the process of satisfying. Callicles in this statement (494a6–7) must mean the process not the state.

16. Benson 1990 makes the correct point that from Callicles' claim that "every . . . appetite is painful" it does not logically follow that he holds that *only* appetites are painful. Thus, although all felt appetites are painful, it is logically consistent to interpret Calliclean appetite as *any* subset of what I have called felt appetites. But this logical point makes no serious criticism of my account, unless one were willing to claim that there are reasonable—in addition to merely logical—grounds to assert that Callicles would classify some of the set of felt appetites as appetites but not others. As things stand, it remains unreasonable to imagine Callicles saying that whether or not this craving I now have for potato chips is an appetite depends on whether or not they physiologically fill an objective need.

17. This objection comes from Gosling and Taylor (1982: 73).

18. For this objection I am in debt to correspondence with Nicholas D. Smith.

19. I am grateful to Roslyn Weiss, as I understood her in discussion, for reinstating the objection of Gosling and Taylor in this way.

20. For instance, in Trollope's *The Small House at Allington*, when Crosbie's strong desire to marry Alexandrina is satisfied, he is worse off.

21. This problem is similar to one Kripke (1972: 45, n. 13) raises for Lewis's counterpart theory.

22. For example, in Trollope's *The Small House at Allington*, Bell does not expect or desire to receive three thousand pounds from the squire, but finds it a good.

23. For example, Fred Astaire and Ginger Rogers in the movie *Easter Parade*.

24. Putnam likewise apparently recognizes the possibility of a similar experience in his distinction between "real" and "notional" opinions (1981: 127); presumably he would recognize the same distinction about desire.

25. See Penner 1988 and 1991 and Brickhouse and Smith (1994: 73–92) for discussion of these and other such passages in the Socratic dialogues.

26. Stampe 1987 argues persuasively that desire can possess "per se authority," that is, the capacity to make something intrinsically good and hence worthy of rational pursuit. See especially his example of the weekend German student, p. 198. It is arguable that both Aristotle (*NE* VI.2) and Hume (*Treatise* II.2) recognized this capacity of desire.

27. It is essentially this strategy that Philonous uses on Hylas's distinction between true and felt sensible objects, in Berkeley's *Three Dialogues*. Gosling and Taylor (1982: 40–41) attribute similar skeptical considerations as a motive for a hedonism of the moment to a near-contemporary of Callicles, Aristippus.

28. Hume, *Treatise* III.1; Weber (1978: 69–98), Popper (1959: 37–38, 53–54); see also discussion of Popper in Laudan (1984: 47–50).

29. See MacIntyre's discussion of emotivism (1984: 18–35).

Chapter 5

1. Of the interpreters I consider, only Dodds 1959 finds both arguments defensible. But there are problems with the first argument on his interpretation (see note 9 below), and objections to the second that he has not considered.

2. I am in debt to Nicholas D. Smith, who drew my attention to this problem.

3. Some interpreters take Socrates' relation to be nothing but mutual exclusion in a subject, for example Dodds (1959: 310), Irwin (1977: 311, 1979: 201–202) and Gosling and Taylor (1982: 72). Others take Socrates' relation to be mutual exclusion and incapacity for a subject simultaneously to become rid of both, for example Santas (1979: 268) and Kahn (1983: 107). As we shall see below, this addition does not strengthen the relation of mutual exclusion; it is a mere consequence of it.

4. A similar distinction reconciles this refutation of Callicles with *Lys.* 216d–217b, where Socrates postulates things "which are neither bad nor good."

5. Socrates' argument is given this sort of formulation by Irwin and Gosling and Taylor; neither object to the inference to conclusion *c*. For Irwin, this is his inference to "the presence of pleasure is not identical with doing well," which he says "follows" in 1977: 311, and does not question in 1979: 201–202. For Gosling and Taylor (1982: 72) it is the inference to "those cases of feeling pleasure are not cases of being benefited." Although Gosling and Taylor (1982: 73) do not object to this inference, they claim not to be raising all the objections "which a full discussion would require."

6. This strategy was suggested to me by Nicholas D. Smith.

7. This is the implicit interpretation of W. D. Woodhead's translation in Hamilton and Cairns 1961; he translates a Greek plural (not dual) demonstrative as "pair" in Socrates' summary of his argument at 497d5–7. Santas (1979: 268) gives the same

reading to 497d5–7, and seems to understand the argument as showing a non-identity of pairs.

8. This is the strategy of Dodds (1959: 309), followed by Kahn (1983: 107).

9. It is not possible for Dodds 1959, who formulates the argument in terms of opposites, to brush off the distinction. For the relation he has picked out, "incapacity for coexistence," that is, mutual exclusion in a subject (p. 310), fails to separate (1) the opposites or (2) the requisites: (1) doing well cannot coexist with doing poorly, but neither can the satisfaction of drinking coexist with dissatisfaction of not drinking. Again, (2) doing well can coexist with the desire to do well; likewise the satisfaction of drinking can coexist with thirst.

10. Socrates uses this insight to refute such definitions of virtue as quietness (*Chrm.* 159b–160d), endurance (*La.* 192b–193d), confidence (*Prt.* 350b), and honesty (*Rep.* I 331b–d); as well as such candidates for the title "good possessions" as health and wealth (*Euthyd.* 281b–d).

11. I have adopted here the counter-factual reasoning of the sort made in *Hp. Mi.* 376a–b.

12. Kahn (1983: 109, n. 57) sees this argument as "only a more fully stated version" of the two counter-examples. To appreciate the philosophical necessity of this second refutation after the two counter-examples, one must see (1) that the two counter-examples, though effective refutations of Callicles' view of the good life, fail to refute his philosophic identity thesis (indeed, Callicles does not even formally commit himself to the identity thesis until after the two counter-examples, 495b and 495d), and (2) that this second refutation makes good that failure.

13. The pleased coward also recalls the conclusion of *Prt.*, where maximal pleasure was precisely what distinguished the coward from the courageous. The sort of situation that distinguishes the two is not when the enemy retreats (see also *Grg.* 498a7–8) but when it approaches and attacks, as Laches attests in his definition, *La.* 190e. And it is then that knowledge, not felt appetite, will be crucial in determining maximal pleasure, according to the prudential hedonism of *Prt.* For further discussion of premise 1a, see Dodds (1959: 314), Irwin (1977: 121), Santas (1979: 278–284), and Kahn (1983: 108–109).

14. Irwin says no in 1977: 311; and 1979: 203; but not in 1995: 107–108.

15. I am following Kahn 1983 here, who states that Socrates' second argument points to a "quite general objection to any hedonistic attempt to define personal excellence or morality in terms of the subjective quality of the agent's experience" (pp. 109–10). He goes on to state Aristotle's remark. But Kahn does not take the next step of allowing Socrates to be a hedonist: "in Socrates' view, there is no place for pleasure as an independent criterion of what is admirable [or good]" (p. 93; see also Kahn 1996: 240–242). Thus Kahn must wrestle with the evidence in *Grg.* that Socrates is a hedonist (p. 93 and see following note) and ignore *Prt.*

16. The key premise in the refutation of Polus at 474d3–475a4 rests on a strictly utilitarian hedonism. See Kahn (1983: 93), Tarrant (1994: 116–118), and Solbakk (n.d.). Tarrant 1994 also discusses the evidence of *Hp. Ma.* Further evidence for a prima facie case that Socrates was a hedonist is in Barnes 1991.

Chapter 6

1. A further problem for Brickhouse and Smith (1989: 260) is their use of Socrates' self-deprecatory remarks at 40a1 as evidence that Socrates is better described as having a "chat between friends" than as advancing an argument. The problem is this: they take seriously, as they should, Socrates' argument from the great sign (*Ap.* 40a2–c3). But that argument is included in what Socrates calls "chat" (*Ap.* 39e5). I do not see how they can consistently take one argument but not the other to aim at conviction by putting weight on a preface directed equally at both.

It should be clear that, although my discussion criticizes the reading of this particular argument given by Brickhouse and Smith and Reeve, it nonetheless supports the following general claims made by both interpretations (Brickhouse and Smith 1989: viii; Reeve 1989: xiii): (1) Socrates sincerely tried to win his release at his trial. (2) Socrates intended the arguments he presented at his trial to be taken seriously as such. (3) Socrates' arguments are not to be explained away as irony or rhetoric.

2. I am indebted to Ronald Polansky for this assessment of the views of commentators.

3. For the distinction in the context of Greek philosophy, see Gosling and Taylor (1982: 175). Aristotle restricts modal pleasures to things that are done by a subject; in my definition of modal pleasure I have included also things that happen to a subject. For English philosophy's failure to mark any such distinction between modal and sensate until the time of Gilbert Ryle and C. D. Broad, see Wright (1963: 63–64).

4. Roochnik (1985: 215) provides two further ad hominem objections why Socrates cannot call sleep a gain. First, Socrates thinks it is good for him to waken Athens from its slumbers by being a gadfly to it. So he must think that sleep without waking is undesirable. But "awake," in this context, is a metaphor. Socrates does not literally believe Athens is asleep. What he means by this figure of speech is that it has been good for Socrates to goad the Athenians to change for the better, in particular to change from a concern for the body to a concern for the soul (29d–e). It is consistent for Socrates on the one hand to want to change the object of Athenians' care and on the other to regard undisturbed sleep as a marvelous good.

Roochnik's second ad hominem is that Socrates in *Symp.* and the long night of conversation which is *Rep.* shows he himself does not need or value sleep. This objection would carry some force if Socrates had claimed that sleep is an unsurpassed good, but he makes that claim only for cross-examination of the dead in an afterlife. That I tend to prefer steak to lobster dinners does not entail that I do not regard a lobster dinner as a gain, and likewise that Socrates occasionally prefers a long conversation to a night's sleep does not entail that he does not regard sleep as a gain.

5. *Chrm.* 159b–160d, 160e–161b, 161b–162a, 163e–164c, 173a–175e; *La.* 192c–d, 192d–193d.

6. For discussion of Socrates' religion, see McPherran (1996: 272–291), who analyses evidence that Socrates argued from cosmological design to the existence of a good and powerful god.

7. This reconstruction has been helped enormously by the conversation and correspondence of Nicholas D. Smith. Indeed, if I only were sure he agreed, I would identify him as co-author of it.

8. Sisyphus and Tantalus are preoccupied by their sufferings, too much so, presumably, to engage in conversation. See Homer, *Od.* XI lines 582–600.

9. I have understood David Sherry and Nicholas D. Smith to have raised versions of this objection.

Chapter 7

1. The Epicurean tradition also claims that nothing besides sensate pleasure is intrinsically good. Goldstein has not made this additional claim.

2. Penner (1987: 80–86), interpreting Moore (1903: 43), has doubts, which I share, about the Moorean repudiation of the "naturalistic fallacy" that Goldstein has adopted.

3. Goldstein (1980: 357–358) explicitly repudiates a related argument attributed to Epicurus, which adds the premise that animals' pleasure-seeking and pain-avoiding behavior is done "by the promptings of nature and apart from reason." For Goldstein, there is a "rational insight" about pleasure and pain, however "simple and basic," which is more than instinctual.

4. See Mooradian 1995 for the importance of this analogy to other aspects of Plato's philosophy. Plato's account of pleasure and pain in *Phlb.* is famously representational. See for example Penner 1971 and Frede 1993. Incidentally, Aristotle also accepts that at least some sorts of pleasures and pains, namely, emotions, are representational. See for example Frede 1996 and Nussbaum 1996.

5. These mistaken appearances are often studied in literature. Consider, for example, the appearances of the pleasures of marriage, as when Crosbie achieves his much anticipated pleasure of enjoying the status of being joined to the family of a lord by marriage to his daughter in Trollope's *The Small House at Allington.*

6. Griffin (1986: 93–105) discusses interval, ordinal, and other scales of measurement.

7. The lack of a metric art causes human and divine enmity, according to Socrates at *Euthphr.* 7c–e. Yet Socrates believes that, although human beings lack it, the gods possess wisdom (*Ap.* 23a–b), which I identify with this metric art. On my interpretation, then, it seems that the gods both possess and lack the metric art. This contradiction is avoided if we notice that the lack must be attributed to Euthyphro's gods, who quarrel and hate, but not to Socrates' gods, who do no such things (*Euthphr.* 6a–c; see also *Rep.* II 377e–378c).

8. See Nussbaum (1986: 458–459) for a summary of the textual evidence.

9. There were, for example, such common expressions as *axion logou,* "worth mentioning" (for example at *Ap.* 23b9; *La.* 183d7, 188c8, 189a1, 190a7; *Prt.* 342e2; *Grg.* 472b8, 510c7; *Rep.* I 348d9). (All translations in this note and the following paragraph in the text are adapted from Cooper 1997.) The etymology suggests a "weight of speech," from the marketplace use of weights to purchase a quantity of something, in this case words: you do or are, or fail to do or be, something with enough weight

which, placed in one scale of the balance, would pull up a speech in the other scale, thereby entitling you to purchase it. In this expression, the metaphor of weight might have been invisible to the Greek speaker. Other such common expressions where the metaphor of weight may have been invisible are *axion oudenos*, "worthless" (*Ap.* 23a7, 38a8, 41e7; *Chrm.* 175e4; *Grg.* 485c7, 488b1, 489c5, 492c8, 514c6, 520a2, 527e7); *axion oligou*, "worth little" (*Ap.* 23a7, *Grg.* 497b7); and *pollou axia*, "worth much" (*Cri.* 46b1, *La.* 182c3). The etymology again suggests a marketplace balance in which a deed or person or thing is put in one scale and is able to pull up nothing, little, or much in the other scale. We find the same metaphor in expressions such as *axiôs andros agathou*, "worthy of a good man" (*Ap.* 32e3); *epainou axios*, "worthy of praise" (*Chrm.* 160a10); *axion tou onomatos*, "worthy of the name" (*Chrm.* 165e2, *La.* 179d5); *axios episkepseôs*, "worthy of examination" (*La.* 197e3); *toutou tou axiômatos axion*, "worthy of this dignity" (*Prt.* 337e1); *pollou epainou axion*, "worthy of much praise" (*Grg.* 526a4). Not just objects but also actions can be purchased in this metaphor, as in expressions such as *axion phrontizein*, "worth thinking about" (*Cri.* 44c7–8); *axion zên*, "worth living" (*Cri.* 53c4–5); *axiôn pisteuesthai*, "worth trusting" (*La.* 181b6); *axion epicheirein manthanein*, "worth trying to learn" (*La.* 184b3); *axioi proestanai*, "think worthy to lead" (*La.* 197d7); *kalos axios akousai*, "worthy to be called beautiful" (*Lys.* 207a2); *axion . . . episkepsasthai*, "worthy to be examined" (*Prt.* 349e1); *axion dialegesthai*, "worthy to discuss" (*Grg.* 461a4); *axion suggnômên echein*, "worthy to be forgiven" (*Grg.* 465e3); *axiôn tô(i) sômati ischurisasthai*, "worthy to have physical strength" (*Grg.* 489c5–6); *axion agasthai*, "worthy to be enthusiastically admired" (*Grg.* 526a3); *axion theasasthai*, "worthy to be viewed" (*Rep.* I 328a7); and *axioi an pleonektein*, "would think worthy to have more" (*Rep.* I 349b8, b10, c1, c4, c6, e12). As I said, these marketplace weight-balance metaphors were perhaps invisible in ordinary Greek usage, just as the marketplace metaphor "worthy" may be invisible in English (notice however that the English word *worthy*, unlike the Greek *axion*, is not a weight metaphor). There are other cases where the weight balance is metaphorical and perhaps invisibly so, but the marketplace is literal, in expressions such as *axiôs tou misthou kai eti pleionos*, "worthy of the fee and still more" (*Prt.* 328b3); *hosou axia einai ta mathêmata*, "how much the lessons are worth" (*Prt.* 328c1); *misthon axiôsas arnusthai*, "think worthy to receive a fee" (*Prt.* 349a4).

Close to the marketplace weight balance is the judicial weight balance, used metaphorically in sentencing a convict who may be *axios pathein ê apoteisai*, "worthy to suffer or to pay" (*Ap.* 36b5); *axios pathein agathon ti*, "worthy to suffer something good" (*Ap.* 36d1)—when the sentence is "true to one's weight" (*kata tên axian tô(i) alêtheia*, *Ap.* 36d2–3, e2); *axios tou kakou*, "worthy of evil" (*Ap.* 37b4, 38a8); *axion memphesthai*, "worthy of blame" (*Ap.* 41e1); *axion katêgorein*, "worthy of accusation" (*Prt.* 328d1); "worthy of flogging . . . of imprisonment . . . of a fine . . . of exile . . . of death" (*Grg.* 480c8, 481a6, 485c2, and see also *Rep.* I 337d2–5).

The weight metaphor of *axios* cognates cannot always have been invisible. For example, the metric art Socrates postulates at *Prt.* 356d recalls the metaphor of weight visibly used at 355d–e, where a "rude questioner" ridicules the possibility of akrasia as follows:

"So," he will say, "does the good within you outweigh (*axiôn ontôn nikan*) the bad or not?" We will clearly say in reply that the good does not outweigh (*ouk axiôn ontôn*) the bad, for if it did, the person . . . would not have made any mistake. "In virtue of what," he might say, "does the good outweigh (*anaxia*) the bad or the bad the good? Only in that one is greater and one is smaller, or more and less."

And we see Socrates using a metaphor of relative weights on a balance beam— weight "against" something—in two passages. "The wisest man knows that weighed against wisdom he is nothing" (*oudenos axios esti . . . pros sophian, Ap.* 23b3–4). Polus's refutation "weighed against the truth is nothing" (*oudenos axios esti pros tên alêtheian, Grg.* 471e7–472a1). Cephalus, an ordinary Greek speaker, uses the same *axios . . . pros* construction in the *Republic*: he says that "weighed against this [sc. sweet hope in the heart for a decent afterlife] the possession of wealth is largest" (*pros dê touto . . . tên tôn chrêmatôn ktêsin pleistou axian einai,* 331a10–11).

The *axios . . . pros* construction is rare in Greek. A search in the electronic *Thesaurus Linguae Graecae* of non-Platonic Attic authors of the fourth and fifth century turned up only two occurrences, both in Aristotle: *pros chrêmath' hê axia metreitai,* "worth measured against money" (*NE* 1164b4); *axia pros tên toutôn huperochên,* "worth against the surpassing [worth of the universe]" (*De Mundo* 391b2).

10. For further discussion of the maximizer/optimizer distinction, see the discussion of premise 1 in chapter 8.

11. On actualizations see Penner 1970.

Chapter 8

1. I prefer the word *righteous* to the alternatives—*moral* and *just*—as a translation of *dikaios*. The Greek adjective connotes a virtue (hence a problem with the translation *moral*). And (unlike *just*) it connotes the general human virtue as well as the specific social virtue. Moreover, only *righteous* provides distinct cognates for two Greek cognates of *dikaios, dikaiosunê* ("righteousness") and *dikê* ("right").

2. I could find no careful examination of the argument that defends its validity. Taylor (1929: 269–270) endorses the lemma but neither considers the many objections one might raise to it nor discusses the subsequent argument and corollary. Lycos 1987 defends the lemma as "successful" "within its limited scope" (p. 121) but it turns out that "successful" does not mean *valid*: at least one inference in the lemma is "not valid" (p. 133). And the subsequent argument, for Lycos, contains an inference that "raises some difficult problems which Socrates leaves unexamined" (p. 145) so that his assessment of the argument is that it leaves us still with the "need to be shown that the person with the just soul who lives well is the person who lives justly in the *ordinary* sense of that expression" (p. 152)—which is in effect what the argument purports to prove.

But Taylor and Lycos are unusual. More typical reactions to the argument are that it is "almost embarrassingly bad" (Cross and Woozley 1966: 52) and "weak and unconvincing to an amazing degree" (Annas 1981: 50). Gutglueck (1988: 22) reports and appears to share these reactions.

3. For one example of how I focus, see n. 4 below.

4. As Gutglueck (1988: 24) points out, Socrates uses a wide range of expressions in the argument: *ethelein*, "to wish" or "be willing"; *axioun*, "to deem worthy"; *hêgeisthai dikaion einai*, "to think it right"; *boulesthai*, "to desire"; and *hamillasthai hôs*, "to compete so [that]." In addition to these my own term "attempts" captures the conative sense that *pleonektei* must carry at 349c12.

Gutglueck believes that this "bewildering variety of expressions" raises a problem for Socrates' argument. For, he claims, all these expressions, "if they are to satisfy the logical requirements of the argument, must convey the same meaning" (pp. 23–24). "If . . . the sense of any one locution should prove to diverge irreconcilably from that of its collateral terms, this inconsistency of language would then entail an inconsistency of meaning, and the argument would necessarily be vitiated on that score" (p. 24). This claim is false. For an argument to be invalid due to the fallacy of equivocation, it needs not only to use a range of distinct meanings, but to trade on them illegitimately. There is no fallacy—indeed it multiplies the argument—if rather than a single meaning there is a range of meanings for each of which unequivocally the entire argument is sound. For ease of exposition I have focused on just one such meaning, "attempts," which I define in n. 7.

Lycos (1987: 120–136) reads Socrates' argument to concern motives. This is a defect in his reading, for not only is "motive" not among the range of expressions that Socrates uses, the sense of "motive" is not a sense in which the argument is sound, as Lycos himself notices (p. 133; see also n. 20 below).

5. I thank Rick Creath for these felicitous terms.

6. Let *F* and *G* be *adjectivals* (that is, adjectives or adjectival phrases). Then being *F* (the supervening property) *supervenes* on being *G* (the base property) just in case we can logically or causally infer that if something is *G*, it is *F*. One consequence of supervenience is that two things cannot differ in their supervening properties without differing in their base properties. Supervening properties need be neither identical with nor constituted by base properties. (In this definition and remarks I follow Brink 1989: 160.)

7. Objection: the physician's motive as a physician need not be to have more than a non-physician, nor need a non-physician's motive be to have more than a physician. Reply: Let me distinguish "motive" and "intent" from "attempt." An example will illustrate the difference. Oedipus attempted (and succeeded in his attempt) to marry his mother, but it was neither his motive nor intent to do so. In general, the difference may be stated as follows. In a sentence of the form, "*P* attempts *A*," we may substitute any expression that is extensionally equivalent with *A* salva veritate. But in a sentence of the form "*P* intends *A*" or "*P's* motive is *A*," we may not so substitute. In Quine's (1953: 142) phrase, the contexts "intends that . . ." and "motive is . . ." are "referentially opaque," but the context "attempts that . . ." is referentially transparent.

8. Reeve (1988: 20) might be understood to be making this claim: "The fact that the Unjust man tries to 'outdo' everyone in the sense of trying to get the better of them does not in the least show that Injustice is not a Skill—practitioners of competitive Skills, such as Generalship or Boxing, do it all the time."

9. Let *S*, *O*, and *O′* be as defined above. Then *pleonexia* relative to *O* or *O′* is the disposition to attempt to have more *O* or *O′* than everyone else, both those who are counterparts and those who are contradictories with reference to *S*.

10. The objection might be made that there are two types of ignorance of skill: (1) ignorance of the identity or constituents of the object of that skill's actions, and (2) ignorance of the means to the object of that skill's actions. An example of the first type of ignorance would be a case where a lyre-string tuner confuses *tuned* with *tightest* string. In this type, there is a necessary confusion of the object with something else. An example of the second type of ignorance would be a case where a lyre-tuner knows what a tuned string should sound like (for perhaps she plays the pipe in perfect pitch) but does not know how to adjust the string's peg to produce that tone. In this type of ignorance there is no necessary confusion of the object with something else.

The shortest reply to this objection is to concede it and revise the argument so that it is concerned only with the first type of ignorance. Thus in premise 1b let us revise "ignorant of (knowledgeable in) *S*" to "ignorant (knowledgeable) of the identity or constituents of the object of *S*". Since, as we shall see in the discussion of premise 2, the disagreements between the righteous and the unrighteous have to do with the identity or constituents of the object of their shared characteristic activity, the revised argument will be sound.

A subtler, and I believe more Socratic, reply would distinguish the *tuner's art* (which our piper possesses) from some distinct mechanical skill governing the manipulation of wooden pegs and strings. Such an art, strictly, is subordinate to tuning, not identical with it.

11. Annas (1981: 52) appears to think that Socrates' argument must be interpreted as begging the question in this way against Thrasymachus: "Thrasymachus is not given the chance to protest, but surely should have said that the analogy does not hold. Injustice is not a hamhanded attempt to do what justice succeeds at doing." Likewise Cross and Woozley (1966: 52–53): "There is no reason at all for thinking of the unjust man as a second-rate or third-rate version of a just man, as the bad musician is of the good musician." Irwin (1977: 181–182, but not in 1995: 177–178), also charges Socrates with begging the question on this point.

12. The word is introduced by Thrasymachus at 344c8, where he takes it to be equivalent to "advantaging" (*sumpheron*), which is the word used in Thrasymachus's original definition of "righteous" (338c2, reiterated by him at 341a4 and 344c7).

13. Thus we have an explanation why Thrasymachus does not protest this feature of Socrates' argument: he cannot, given his own agreement with Socrates as to the whole point of their discussion. Hence Socrates' argument at this point is dialectically effective against Thrasymachus.

14. See Annas (1981: 54): "It is often said that the argument is fallacious because it trades on an ambiguity in 'live well': between living in an efficient and well-ordered way, and living a virtuous life." Annas herself believes that this ambiguity cannot "be located in a single word."

15. Nettleship (1937: 42), cited by Cornford (1941: 37), makes a similar connection between righteousness and self-interest as the one I have attempted: "When men are agreed that a certain sort of conduct constitutes virtue, if they mean anything at all, they must mean that in that conduct man finds happiness."

16. Notice that we might raise a parallel objection as we did to the first premise 1*a*. The objection there was that the expert as such does not act from a motive of having

more than the non-expert; here it is that the righteous as such do not have as their motive self-interest; in particular they have no motive of seeking to have more than the unrighteous. This objection, here as at n. 7 above, is met by distinguishing *motive* from *attempt*.

17. It might be objected that sometimes the ignorant do well by luck. The reply is that luck is not a significant factor in skills or skill-like activities of high degrees of complexity, such as are at issue here, as Penner (1991: 164, n. 18) points out.

18. Allan (1944: 106) objects to Socrates' argument: "It is evidently untrue that things alike in one respect are alike in all. Yet unless this is meant, the argument falls to the ground." Likewise Shorey (1933: 213). In my reading of the premise I have avoided this problem by following Lycos (1987: 135): "The claim that 'a thing is what the thing it resembles is as such' seems to state, in a rather compressed form, the methodological rule of probable inference."

19. See Copi and Burgess-Jackson 1992, ch. 5, esp. pp. 198–199, for exposition of this rule.

20. Lycos (1987: 133) objects to this inference: "Socrates' inference . . . is not valid. . . . [M]ay it not be the case that there are some who can live wise and good lives without having the antipleonectic motive characteristic of craft-knowledge?" My defense of its validity escapes this problem, since it attributes an attempt, but no particular motive, to the righteous. See n. 7 above.

21. Notice (as pointed out by for example Annas 1981: 53–54) that not only artifacts have functions, according to this definition.

22. White (1979: 72) objects: "In 353e Plato alludes to prior agreement that justice is a virtue or excellence of the soul. (The ensuing argument seems to rely, illegitimately, on something stronger than this, namely that justice is *the* single virtue or excellence of the soul.)" Likewise Cross and Woozley (1966: 58): "Thrasymachus's mistake was to have agreed with Socrates that justice is the excellence of the soul. Also Irwin (1977: 182): "[Justice] has not been shown to be the virtue that contributes to happiness" (see also Irwin 1995: 179). And Annas (1981: 55): "Socrates says, astoundingly, 'Now we have agreed that justice is excellence of soul, and that injustice is vice of soul?' 'We have so agreed,' says Thrasymachus. But where? and how? Presumably Thrasymachus is referring to the outcome of the first argument, but that is not precisely what was proved there. . . . [T]his matters. For the whole argument depends on this premise, and collapses if it is not accepted. Yet it has not been argued for."

23. Brickhouse and Smith (1994: 115) make Aristotle's criticism. Annas (1981: 54) has a different objection to this inference: "Plato says blithely, 'so the just soul and the just man will live well, and the unjust man badly.' However, what lives well is the just *man*, but what the argument was about was the just *soul*. Ultimately, Plato believes that a person *is* his soul, so he sees no gap because he sees no ultimate gap between talking of a person and talking of his soul. But here this is a very strong assumption to make, and we have seen not a glimmer of argument for it so far." My defense of the inference does not make the assumption that a person is his soul.

24. It may be objected that a shorter life keeps one from living well, on the grounds that it is a deprivation. But this is not an objection to the validity of the inference

under consideration; it is an independent argument to a contradictory conclusion (which may, however, help to explain why most people find the argument's conclusion unacceptable). See section 6.3 for discussion of deprivation of conscious activity as a bad thing.

Chapter 9

1. The conflict has been noticed by for example Kraut (1984: 38, n. 21), Irwin (1992: 215), and Brickhouse and Smith 1994, who give the conflicting passages the most thorough discussion. Brickhouse and Smith 1994 are convinced of the soundness of Aristotle's criticism that activity is needed and mere possession insufficient. Accordingly, philosophical charity makes them reluctant to attribute the sufficiency thesis to Socrates (likewise, apparently, Striker 1994: 244–245). I argued in section 8.2 that Aristotle's criticism fails; hence such charity is misplaced.

2. When premise 5 is stipulated in addition to premises 1 and 2, the problems raised are just as acute for Brickhouse and Smith as for the interpretation they attack. They surely cannot rely on the cases of virtuous opposition to tyranny or compliance with religious doctrine to establish the wretchedness of such a life. For they rightly hold that virtuous activity ensures happiness ("The only exceptions to the general point that the virtuous are happy are those who suffer from such severe external impediments that they are unable to act on their moral goodness," Brickhouse and Smith 1994: 118–119), and both the opposition and compliance presumed by premise 5 are, by hypothesis, cases of virtuous activity.

3. Brickhouse and Smith (1994: 119) make this claim. These passages can be made to entail the insufficiency by adding another assumption, namely, premise 5 above. In that case the passages count equally against the Brickhouse and Smith interpretation that for Socrates virtuous activity is sufficient for happiness.

4. Brickhouse and Smith point out that the question leading to this assertion is ambiguous (1994: 117 n. 27). We may admit this, but the assertion itself is unambiguous.

5. I have a quibble here. They claim that *Hp. Mi.* 366b7–c3 shows that when Socrates makes a general point, he ignores counter-examples that would follow from cases of illness or impairment (1994: 119, fn. 29). The passage they cite shows just the opposite. He does not ignore such counter-examples; he explicitly mentions them to set them apart from consideration of the general point he is making there. Their interpretation that he is tacitly setting aside such cases in *Grg.* and *Rep.* thus gains no support from the *Hp. Mi.* passage they cite; to the contrary, that passage counts against their interpretation.

6. A final quibble with Brickhouse and Smith (1994: 119, n. 31): I side with Reeve against their interpretation of *Euthyd.* 280b2–3. That is, I take it that the passage does commit Socrates and Cleinias to the view—which Brickhouse and Smith consider to be absurd—that no misfortune can ever befall the wise person. The view is not absurd if we allow that wisdom is the sort of thing no human will ever attain, the sort of thing only a god may have. And this is undeniably Socrates' view of wisdom

("In reality the god is wise . . . [and the oracle is saying:] 'O human beings, the man among you is wisest who, like Socrates, knows that in respect of wisdom he is in truth of no value'" *Ap.* 23a5–b4.)

7. Irwin concludes that the Socratic texts are incoherent (1992: 213–214).

Chapter 10

1. An important exception is Brickhouse and Smith (1994: 112–123; see ch. 9).

2. Irwin (1977: 92–93) defends the view that virtue is only instrumentally good. But in light of the criticisms of Vlastos (1984: 207, n. 54) and Zeyl (1982), Irwin (1986: 201, 1995: 67–68) is more hesitant. On my reading, the mere possession of virtue is merely instrumentally valuable; the activity of virtue is also, as pleasant activity, intrinsically valuable (see section 8.2).

3. The first alternative is held by for example Hackforth (1928: 42) and Nussbaum (1986), the second by for example Vlastos (1969) and Zeyl (1989).

4. This distinction is in Aristotle, *NE* I.1 1094a2–5; in Plato, *Rep.* II 357b–d; and is suggested by the Socratic distinction at *Grg.* 467c–468a and aporia at *Lys.* 218d–222e.

5. This precision is observed by Socrates at *Rep.* I 341c–d and 345c–d.

6. Objection: There are other pleasant activities besides virtuous activities; Socrates cannot convincingly ignore them. Reply: weaving may be my pleasure as a weaver, theft as a thief, and so forth. But only virtue is my pleasure as a human being. I cannot here give further discussion of the problem of the relationship of virtuous activity to other skillful activity or of human life as a whole to its parts.

7. Virtue is needed for any benefit: *Euthyd.* 281b5–6. Brickhouse and Smith (1994: 133–134) question this interpretation but even so cannot escape the problem of the demon, to be raised presently. For even they need to explain why virtue is always preferable. They give three reasons.

1. A life under guidance of wisdom is of greater value than one composed of a series of lucky guesses, felicitous yet systematic mistakes, or consistently bungled attempts at viciousness. For understanding why one's actions are correct is a good over and above the correctness of the actions themselves, and the possession of virtue entails an understanding of why what its possessor does is correct.

2. Socrates' demon does not allow him to draw authoritative inferences regarding what course of action would express moral virtue. And non-virtuous people are unlikely always to perform virtuous actions (because of their epistemic deficiency). Socrates' demon at best keeps him from vicious actions; it does not guarantee virtuous as opposed to merely non-vicious and non-virtuous actions.

3. Virtue provides its possessor with the ability to transform all potential (dependent) goods into actual goods, to make the most of opportunities.

Accordingly, they face these problems: Reason 1 is at odds with the picture they give of the value of virtue, namely, that its value is entirely a matter of the results of activities. (They say: "what qualifies the good person as being 'blessed and happy' is the fact that he or she succeeds in his or her actions," p. 114). So reason 1 must be discounted. Reasons 2 and 3, moreover, are insufficient to demonstrate the advantages of the possession of virtue to the possession of a super demon.

8. *Ap.* 40a: an example of the demon at work is found at *Euthyd.* 272e3–4; see also *Thg.* 128d–130e.

Bibliography

Allan, D. J. 1944. *Plato: Republic Book I*. 2nd ed. London: Methuen.

Annas, J. 1981. *An Introduction to Plato's Republic*. Oxford: Clarendon.

Anton, John P., and Anthony Preus, eds. 1989. *Plato (Essays in Ancient Greek Philosophy* III). Albany: State University of New York Press.

Armleder, Paul J. 1966. "Death in Plato's *Apologia*," *Classical Bulletin* 42: 46.

Austin, J. L. 1979. "A Plea for Excuses," in Urmson and Warnock 1979: 175–204.

Barnes, Jonathan. 1991. "Socrates the Hedonist," in Boudouris 1991: 22–32.

Belgum, Eunice. 1990. *Knowing Better: An Account of Akrasia*. New York: Garland.

Benson, Hugh H. 1990. "Comment on Rudebusch's 'Callicles' Hedonism,'" paper read to the Pacific Division Meeting of the American Philosophical Association, Los Angeles.

———, ed. 1992. *Essays on the Philosophy of Socrates*. New York: Oxford University Press.

Berman, Scott. 1991a. "How Polus Was Refuted: Reconsidering Plato's *Gorgias* 474c–475c," *Ancient Philosophy* 11: 265–284.

———. 1991b. "Socrates and Callicles on Pleasure," *Phronesis* 36: 117–140.

Boudouris, Konstantine J., ed. 1991. *Proceedings of the Second International Conference on Greek Philosophy: The Philosophy of Socrates*. Athens: International Association for Greek Philosophy.

Brandis, Christian. 1835. *Handbuch der Geschichte der Griechisch-Romisch Philosophie* I. Berlin: Reimer.

Brickhouse, Thomas C., and Nicholas D. Smith. 1989a. *Socrates on Trial*. Princeton: Princeton University Press.

———. 1989b. "A Matter of Life and Death in Socratic Philosophy," *Ancient Philosophy* 9: 155–165.

———. 1994. *Plato's Socrates*. New York: Oxford University Press.

Brink, D. O. 1989. *Moral Realism and the Foundations of Ethics*. Cambridge: Cambridge University Press.

Burnet, John, ed. 1900–1907. *Platonis Opera*. Oxford: Clarendon.

Cleary, John J., ed. 1988. *Proceedings of the Boston Area Colloquium in Ancient Philosophy* III. Lanham: University Press of America.

Cohen, Maurice. 1962. "The Aporias in Plato's Early Dialogues," *Journal of the History of Ideas* 23: 163–174.

Cooper, John M., ed., and D. S. Hutchinson, associate ed. 1997. *Plato: Complete Works*. Indianapolis: Hackett.

Copi, I. M., and K. Burgess-Jackson. 1992. *Informal Logic*. 2d ed. New York: Macmillan.

Cornford, F. M. 1941. *The Republic of Plato*. New York: Oxford University Press.

Crombie, I. M. 1962. *An Examination of Plato's Doctrines*. 2 vols. London: Routledge.

Cross, R. C., and A. D. Woozley. 1966. *Plato's Republic*. New York: St. Martin's.

Davidson, Donald. 1970. "How Is Weakness of Will Possible?" in Feinberg 1970: 93–113. Reprinted in Davidson 1980.

———. 1980. *Essays on Actions and Events*. Oxford: Clarendon.

Dent, N. J. H. 1984. *The Moral Psychology of the Virtues*. Cambridge: Cambridge University Press.

Dodds, E. R. 1951. *The Greeks and the Irrational*. Berkeley: University of California Press.

———. 1959. *Plato: Gorgias*. Oxford: Clarendon.

Ehnmark, Erland. 1946. "Socrates and the Immortality of the Soul," *Eranos* 44: 105–122.

Feinberg, Joel, ed. 1970. *Moral Concepts*. Oxford: Clarendon.

Findlay, J. N. 1961. *Values and Intentions*. New York: Macmillan.

Frede, Dorothea. 1993. *Philebus*. Indianapolis: Hackett.

———. 1996. "Mixed Feelings in Aristotle's *Rhetoric*," in Rorty 1996: 258–285.

Gallop, D. 1964. "The Socratic Paradox in the *Protagoras*," *Phronesis* 9: 117–129.

Goldstein, Irwin. 1980. "Why People Prefer Pleasure to Pain," *Philosophy* 55: 349–362.

———. 1983. "Pain and Masochism," *Journal of Value Inquiry* 17: 219–223.

———. 1985. "Hedonic Pluralism," *Philosophical Studies* 48: 49–55.

———. 1989. "Pleasure and Pain: Unconditional, Intrinsic Values," *Philosophy and Phenomenological Research* 50: 255–275.

———. 1994. "Identifying Mental States: A Celebrated Hypothesis Refuted," *Australasian Journal of Philosophy* 72: 46–62.

Gómez-Lobo, Alfonso. 1994. *The Foundations of Socratic Ethics*. Indianapolis: Hackett.

Gosling, J. C. G., and C. C. W. Taylor. 1982. *The Greeks on Pleasure*. Oxford: Clarendon.

Griffin, J. 1986. *Well-Being: Its Meaning, Measurement, and Moral Importance*. Oxford: Clarendon.

Griswold, Charles. 1985. "Plato's Metaphilosophy," in O'Meara, ed., 1985: 1–33.

Grote, George. 1865. *Plato and the Other Companions of Socrates* I. London: Murray.

Gutglueck, J. 1988. "From *PLEONEXIA* to *POLUPRAGMOSUNÊ*: a Conflation of Possession and Action in Plato's *Republic*," *American Journal of Philology* 109: 20–39.

Guthrie, W. K. C. 1975. *A History of Greek Philosophy* IV. Cambridge: Cambridge University Press.

Hackforth, R. 1928. "Hedonism in Plato's *Protagoras*," *Classical Quarterly* 22: 39–42.

Haden, James. 1983. "Friendship in Plato's *Lysis*," *Review of Metaphysics* 37: 327–356.

Hamilton, Edith, and Huntington Cairns, eds. 1961. *The Collected Dialogues of Plato*. Princeton: Princeton University Press.

Hoerber, Robert J. 1966. "Note on Plato, *Apologia* 42," *Classical Bulletin* 42: 92.

Irwin, T. 1977. *Plato's Moral Theory: The Early and Middle Dialogues*. Oxford: Clarendon.

———. 1979. *Plato: Gorgias*. Oxford: Clarendon.

———. 1986. "Socrates the Epicurean?" *Illinois Classical Studies* 11: 85–112. My page references are to the reprint in Benson 1992: 198–219.

———. 1995. *Plato's Ethics*. Oxford University Press

Jones, E. 1964. *The Life and Work of Sigmund Freud*. Harmondsworth: Penguin.

Kahn, C. H. 1983. "Drama and Dialectic in Plato's *Gorgias*," *Oxford Studies in Ancient Philosophy* 1: 75–121.

———. 1996. *Plato and the Socratic Dialogue: The Philosophical Use of a Literary Form*. Cambridge: Cambridge University Press.

Kraut, Richard. 1984. *Socrates and the State*. Princeton: Princeton University Press.

———. 1994. "Desire and the Human Good," *The Proceedings and Addresses of the American Philosophical Association* 68: 39–54.

Kripke, S. A. 1972. *Naming and Necessity*. Cambridge, Mass.: Harvard University Press.

Laudan, L. 1984. *Science and Values*. Berkeley: University of California Press.

Lee, E. N. , A. Mourelatos, and R. Rorty, eds. 1973. *Exegesis and Argument*. Assen: Van Gorcum.

Lycos, K. 1987. *Plato on Justice and Power*. Albany: State University of New York Press.

MacIntyre, A. 1984. *After Virtue*. 2d ed. Notre Dame: University of Notre Dame Press.

McPherran, Mark L. 1996. *The Religion of Socrates*. University Park: Pennsylvania State University Press.

Mele, Alfred R. 1987. *Irrationality: An Essay on Akrasia, Self-Deception, And Self-Control*. New York: Oxford University Press.

Mooradian, Norman. 1995. "What to Do about False Pleasures of Overestimation? *Philebus* 41a5–42c5," *Apeiron* 28: 91–112.

Moore, George E. 1903. *Principia Ethica*. Cambridge: Cambridge University Press.

Moreau, J. 1939. *La Construction de l'idéalisme platonicien*. Paris: Boivin.

Nagel, T. 1979. "Death," in *Mortal Questions*. Cambridge: Cambridge University Press.

Nails, Debra. 1995. *Agora, Academy, and the Conduct of Philosophy*. Dordrecht: Kluwer. Chapter 4, "The Early Middle Late Consensus: How Deep? How Broad?" is reprinted in Smith 1998.

Nettleship, R. L. 1937. *Lectures on the Republic of Plato*. London: Macmillan.

Nozick, R. 1974. *Anarchy, State, and Utopia*. Oxford: Blackwell.

Nussbaum, Martha. 1986. *The Fragility of Goodness: Luck and Ethics in Greek Tragedy and Philosophy*. Cambridge: Cambridge University Press.

———. 1996. "Aristotle on Emotions and Rational Persuasion," in Rorty 1996: 303–323.

O'Meara, Dominic J., ed. 1985. *Platonic Investigations*. Washington, D.C.: Catholic University of America.

Parfit, D. 1984. *Reasons and Persons*. Oxford: Clarendon.

Penner, Terry. 1970. "Verbs and the Identity of Actions," in Wood and Pitcher 1970.

———. 1971. "False Anticipatory Pleasures: *Philebus 36a3–1a6*," *Phronesis* 10: 166–178.

———. 1973a. "Socrates on Virtue and Motivation," in Lee, Mourelatos and Rorty 1973: 133–151.

———. 1973b. "The Unity of Virtue," *Philosophical Review* 82: 35–68.

———. 1987. *The Ascent from Nominalism: Some Existence Arguments in Plato's Middle Dialogues*. Boston: Reidel.

———. 1988. "Socrates on the Impossibility of Belief-Relative Sciences," in Cleary 1988: 263–325.

———. 1990. "Plato and Davidson: Parts of the Soul and Weakness of Will," in *Canadian Journal of Philosophy*, Supplement 16: 35–74.

———. 1991. "Desire and Power in Socrates," *Apeiron* 24: 147–202.

———. 1992. "Socrates and the Early Dialogues," in Kraut 1992: 121–169.

Popper, K. 1959. *Logic of Scientific Discovery*. New York: Basic Books.

Putnam, H. 1981. *Reason, Truth and History*. Cambridge: Cambridge University Press.

Quine, W. V. O. 1953. "Reference and Modality," page references are to Quine 1980.

———. 1980. *From a Logical Point of View*. Cambridge, Mass.: Harvard University Press.

Reeve, C. D. C. 1988. *Philosopher-Kings*. Princeton: Princeton University Press.

———. 1989. *Socrates in the Apology: An Essay on Plato's Apology of Socrates*. Indianapolis: Hackett.

Richardson, Henry S. 1990. "Measurement, Pleasure, and Practical Science in Plato's *Protagoras*," *Journal of the History of Philosophy* 28: 7–32.

Roochnik, David L. 1985. "*Apology* 40c4–41e7: Is Death Really a Gain?" *Classical Journal* 80: 212–220.

Rorty, Amélie Oksenberg, ed. 1996. *Essays on Aristotle's Rhetoric*. Berkeley: University of California Press.

Rudebusch, George. 1988. "Plato on Knowing a Tradition," *Philosophy East and West* 38: 324–333.

———. 1991. "*Sophist 237–239*," *Southern Journal of Philosophy* 29: 521–531.

Ryle, Gilbert. 1949. *The Concept of Mind*. New York: Barnes and Noble.

Santas, G. 1979. *Socrates: Philosophy in Plato's Early Dialogues*. London: Routledge.

Shorey, P. 1933. *What Plato Said*. Chicago: University of Chicago Press.

Sidgwick, H. 1907. *The Methods of Ethics*. 7th ed. London: Macmillan.

Smith, Nicholas D., ed. 1998. *Plato: Critical Assessments*. London: Routledge.

Smyth, Herbert W. 1956. *Greek Grammar*. Revised from 1920 edition by Gordon M. Messing. Cambridge, Mass.: Harvard University Press.

Solbakk, Jan H. No date. *Forms and Functions of Medical Knowledge in Plato*. Unpublished manuscript.

Sprague, Rosamond Kent. 1962. *Plato's Use of Fallacy*. London: Routledge.

Stampe, D. 1987. "The Authority of Desire," *Philosophical Review* 96: 335–381.

Stocker, Michael. 1990. *Plural and Conflicting Values*. Oxford: Clarendon.

Stokes, Michael C. 1986. *Plato's Socratic Conversations: Drama and Dialectic in Three Dialogues*. London: Athlone.

Striker, Gisela. 1994. "Plato's Socrates and the Stoics," in Waerdt 1994: 241–251.

Sullivan, J. P. 1961. "Hedonism in Plato's *Protagoras*," *Phronesis* 6: 9–28.

Tarrant, Harold A. S. 1994. "The *Hippias Major* and Socratic Theories of Pleasure," in Waerdt 1994: 107–126.

Taylor, A. E. 1929. *Plato: The Man and His Work*. New York: Dial.

Taylor, C. C. W. 1980. "Plato, Hare and Davidson on Akrasia," *Mind* 89: 499–518.

———. 1982. "The End of the *Euthyphro*," *Phronesis* 27: 109–118.

———. 1991. *Plato: Protagoras*, revised ed. Oxford: Clarendon.

Teloh, Henry. 1981. *The Development of Plato's Metaphysics*. University Park: Penn State University Press.

Tigerstedt, Eugene N. 1977. *Interpreting Plato*. Uppsala: Almqvist & Wiksell International.

Unger, P. 1990. *Identity, Consciousness and Value*. New York: Oxford University Press.

Urmson, J. O., and G. J. Warnock, eds. 1979. *Philosophical Papers*. 3rd ed. New York: Oxford University Press.

Vlastos, Gregory. 1969. "Socrates on Acrasia," *Phoenix* 23: 71–88.

———. 1984. "Happiness and Virtue in Socrates' Moral Theory," *Proceedings of the Cambridge Philological Society NS* 30: 181–213.

———. 1991. *Socrates: Ironist and Moral Philosopher*. Ithaca: Cornell University Press.

———. 1994. *Socratic Studies*. Cambridge: Cambridge University Press.

Waerdt, Paul A. V. 1994. *The Socratic Movement*. Ithaca: Cornell University Press.

Watson, G. 1977. "Skepticism About Weakness of Will," *Philosophical Review* 86: 316–339.

Weber, M. 1978. *Max Weber Selections*, W. G. Runciman, ed., E. Matthews, trans. Cambridge: Cambridge University Press.

White, Nicholas P. 1976. *Plato on Knowledge and Reality*. Indianapolis: Hackett.

———. 1979. *A Companion to Plato's Republic*. Indianapolis: Hackett.

Wiggins, D. 1978–79. "Weakness of Will, Commensurability, and the Objects of Deliberation and Desire," *Proceedings of the Aristotelian Society* 79: 251–277.

Wood, O. P., and Pitcher, G., eds. 1970. *Ryle*. Garden City, N.Y.: Anchor.

Woodruff, Paul. 1982. *Plato: Hippias Major*. Indianapolis: Hackett.

Wright, G. H. V. 1963. *The Varieties of Goodness*. London: Routledge.

Yourgrau, Palle. 1987. "The Dead," *Journal of Philosophy* 84: 84–101.

Zeller, Eduard. 1888. *Plato and the Older Academy*, S. F. Alleyne and A. Goodwin, trans. London: Longmans, Green.

Zeyl, D. J. 1982. "Socratic Virtue and Happiness," *Archiv für Geschichte der Philosophie* 14: 225–238.

———. 1989. "Socrates and Hedonism: *Protagoras* 351b–358d," in Anton and Preus 1989: 5–26.

Index of Passages

General Index

Achilles, 20, 21, 73
action
  deliberate, 99–107
  desire-triggered, 102, 108
  versus possession, 111
activity
  leisure, 6, 44, 94, 125
  pleasant, 3–6, 124–128
  skillful, 6, 125, 128
  subordinate, 6
  superordinate, 6
  unimpeded, 5, 6, 72, 79, 125
  virtuous, 3, 6, 7, 98, 118–128
actualization, 94
advantage. *See* benefit
  of injustice, 121
  of pain for survival, 84
  to perplexity, 16
  prudential and moral, 104, 105
  of tyranny or rhetoric, 30
  and unconditional desire, 48
aesthete, 95, 110

afterlife, 73–77
Agamemnon, 20, 86
akrasia, 21–29, 77
Alcibiades, 36, 98
Allan, D., 106 n. 18, 143
amusement, 69
analogy
  craft, 90
anger
  makes knowledge impotent, 21
Annas, J., 98 n. 2, 103 n. 11,
    104 n. 14, 109 n. 21,
    109 n. 22, 111 n. 23
answer
  one-sentence, 12–20, 63, 87, 91,
    115
anticipation, 5, 41, 42, 69, 72
aphorism, 12, 13, 16
apology
  as goal of dialogues, 13
aporetic dialogues, 10, 11, 16
aporia, 10, 12, 16